STUCK

STUCK

How We Are Reverse Born Again

STEVE SHORES

WIPF & STOCK · Eugene, Oregon

STUCK
How We Are Reverse Born Again

Copyright © 2022 Steve Shores. All rights reserved. Except for brief quotations in critical publications or reviews, no part of this book may be reproduced in any manner without prior written permission from the publisher. Write: Permissions, Wipf and Stock Publishers, 199 W. 8th Ave., Suite 3, Eugene, OR 97401.

Wipf & Stock
An Imprint of Wipf and Stock Publishers
199 W. 8th Ave., Suite 3
Eugene, OR 97401

www.wipfandstock.com

PAPERBACK ISBN: 978-1-6667-3454-6
HARDCOVER ISBN: 978-1-6667-9049-8
EBOOK ISBN: 978-1-6667-9050-4

03/18/22

Unless otherwise noted, Scripture quotations are taken from the (NASB®) New American Standard Bible®, copyright © 1960, 1971, 1977, 1995, 2020 by The Lockman Foundation. Used by permission. All rights reserved. www.lockman.org.

Citations marked ESV® are from The ESV Bible (The Holy Bible, English Standard Version®), copyright © 2001 by Crossway, a publishing ministry of Good News Publishers. Used by permission. All rights reserved.

All stories from my counseling practice have been modified to respect privacy and confidentiality.

Dedicated to Susan Shores, my wife

Because you say, "I am rich, and have become wealthy, and have need of nothing," and you do not know that you are wretched and miserable and poor and blind and naked, I advise you to buy from Me gold refined by fire, that you may become rich, and white garments, that you may clothe yourself, and that the shame of your nakedness may not be revealed, and eye salve to anoint your eyes, that you may see. Those whom I love, I reprove and discipline; be zealous therefore, and repent.

(Rev 3:17–19)

Contents

Preface ix

Acknowledgments xiii

Introduction: The Battle 1

Chapter 1 Conundrum 9

Chapter 2 Fulcrum 16

Chapter 3 Momentum 28

Chapter 4 Liberation 37

Chapter 5 Pendulum 43

Chapter 6 Humdrum 52

Chapter 7 Poem 59

Chapter 8 Welcome 73

Chapter 9 *Shalōm*, part 1 77

Chapter 10 *Shalōm*, part 2 90

Conclusion 109

Bibliography 111

Preface

The volumes in this series are a subsection of a theology of discipleship focusing on its relational aspect. From this point of view, the four books function in two ways. First, as a cry of the soul, an alarm bell. They aim to awaken the Christian to a pair of perspectives. The first is that far too often, relationships turn into danger zones where harm is perpetrated instead of love given and received (often, then, relationships are really not relationships of true intimacy but arrangements for getting tasks done, especially the task of self-protection). In the fourth book, *Unstuck*, you will find some thoughts about why I like to think of the books as The Relationship Project. Second, considering relationships from an ecological perspective (as in the second book) exposes the difficulty of connecting and shows how selfishness pollutes relationships. This power to pollute is especially true of a subtle brand of selfishness known in the New Testament as the flesh. I see ecology as more than a relational metaphor; I regard it as literally true that relationships share with nature the same limited ability to process toxins. Like the natural environment, relationships reach a point of saturation where pollutants can no longer be handled, and real harm and pain begin. Unless we develop a proper way to deal with pain, love is eclipsed by the flesh's hijacking the heart into survival mode. The heart becomes stuck in the small-minded story of self-concern. Consequently, a theology of pain will weave in and out of the books.

PREFACE

So, what's the connection with Christian discipleship? Why couldn't the books aim *simply* for the general reader and not just a churchgoing readership? This brings up the second major concern of the books, which is the anemic condition of discipleship in the church (Christian Smith calls this anemia "moral therapeutic deism"[1]). Again, two things to consider: First, when Jesus said, "Love one another, even as I have loved you," and followed this up with "By this all men will know that you are My disciples" (John 13:34–35), he described loving relationships as what makes Christian discipleship credible, as what makes the gospel credible. No love, no gospel. Shuffling in and out of self-protective arrangements with one another makes the church disappear into the world (and in some sense, *from* the world). That is, the church becomes a cultural artifact instead of a counterculturual critique and invitation. Second, the books *do* have applicability to the general reader. One who doesn't identify as a Christian could be challenged by the books to ask himself/herself the question "Do I understand what love is? Where do I get the fuel to love well? *Do* I love well?" Further, some who have had toxic brushes with the church may learn from the books that the church is not meant to be a legalistic obstacle course through which heroic efforts earn points in a pressurized meritocracy, but rather a restful gathering in the generosity of God where anxious striving progressively gives way to grateful self-giving to God and others. That is, Christ's church is meant to be a hint of Home.

Each book spotlights the above concerns from a different angle. The first, *Stuck: How We Are Reverse Born Again*, explores the sneaky power of the flesh to turn relationships into mere arrangements. "Born again to a living hope" (1 Pet 1:3), we too often end up hijacked by the flesh to present a canned Christianity that serves as a placeholder, while deep in the heart our fleshly programming nudges us toward a egocentric drive for preferred outcomes. This is how we get "stuck in our stories," small stories that act as shrink-wrap on the Holy Spirit.

The second book, *Cleanup: How Repentance Restores Relationships*, unpacks the dynamics of the war between flesh and Spirit (Gal

---

1. Smith, *Soul Searching*, 162.

PREFACE

5:17) with an aim to understand the power of repentance to release relationships from the prison of mere interpersonal arrangements. Without repentance, the war inside us expands into Hobbes's "war of all against all"[2] as we contend for what we perceive are limited resources. Repentance delivers us from a scarcity model to a generosity model of living. It opens up the possibility of self-giving.

The third book, *We Hate to Wait: Shedding our Harried Self-Love*, presents the Lord as calling us away from instant gratification and toward learning the joy of enduring in hope. The hope intended is twofold: hope for real growth in Christ to refresh us and others from "canned Christianity," and hope of living "from the future"[3]—i.e., from the warmth and light of "the bright morning star" (Rev 22:16). Enlivened by "the powers of the age to come" (Heb 6:5), we learn that God means for Christian waiting to be intentional, formative, and intimate.

The final book, *Unstuck: Truly Connecting for Deep Discipleship*, takes a look at what must happen inside believers in Christ to make us fit to engage with one another in the sphere of other lords and masters. That is, when spheres of influence other than the kingdom of God dominate our lives, sapping the force of the eternal life God has given us, how can we engage lovingly and truthfully with one another to invite each other to an "exodus" lifestyle, one progressively free from enslavement to the power of "the world forces of this darkness" (Eph 6:12)? Discipleship is to be a self-giving that calls one another away from other masters to recommit to the one who is "Lord of lords" (Rev 19:16).

---

2. Hobbes, *Of Man*, 392.
3. Jones, *Soul Making*, 192.

Acknowledgments

Other than the lordship of Jesus Christ and the faithful influence of my wife, Susan, I am who I've become (with all limitations humbly admitted) through the call to discipleship that has come through my relationship with Dr. Larry Crabb. Larry—impressively supported by his wife, Rachael—helped me over and over again to experience the influence of Paul's prayer that "the eyes of your heart may be enlightened" (Eph 1:18). I have never met another man who sought this God-given enlightenment more passionately than Larry. I have never met another man who, once having found it, sought to live it out with all his soul.

I would also like to thank Kara Barlow, my copy editor. I'm grateful that she has consistently provided a wise and clarifying perspective. Not to mention an eye for detail that I lack. These books would be much the poorer without her.

Introduction: The Battle

I love the church of God. It is Christ's body on earth. The church constitutes our opportunity, in *our* embodied lives, to embody Christ on earth. The amazing truth is that we get to enact Christ's presence in some small way, conveying his freeing truth, healing love, and a kind call to repentance. That's far more astounding a privilege than, say, being given an at bat in the World Series; or being the first woman to be president. Neither of the two belong in the same league with God's giving us new birth and then sending us in a splashdown of spreading his embodied presence on this planet. That puts all earthly honors in the deep shade. To belong to Christ's church is the gift of all gifts.

But God's church also frustrates me. I was struck recently by a sentence that put point to my exasperation: "[The] real enemy remains superstition, which may express itself in a hundred different kinds of practice and theory, but ultimately manifests itself in neglected, corrupted discipleship which fails to press forward into fresh worlds."[1] Superstition implies a state of being overawed by someone or something that doesn't merit the awe. The church exasperates, because it stands too much in awe of the human project. In many of its iterations, the human stands apart from God, looks at itself, and says, "It is we who have made us and not he himself," in a corruption of Ps 100:3. I say the church is overawed by this project because its prophesying against it is weak and its acting as a

---

1. Käsemann, *Perspectives on Paul*, 27.

chaplain for it is too often its prevailing tendency. Because of these weaknesses, the church falls short, vitiating its Founder's story.

One outcome is that the church settles for acting as a giant behavior-modification plant seeking to churn out well-behaved units that fit nicely into mass culture and take their places (or try to) in an ever more precarious job system. The average sermon, even in ostensibly Bible-teaching churches, is designed to shape behavior more than to probe for truth (and lies) "in the innermost being" (Ps 51:6). By devolving into behavior tweaking, the church preaches to the outermost being and ends up being more moralistic than transforming. Moral behavior ladled over unexamined hearts degenerates into secret self-congratulation and a more presentable form of self-seeking. From the church doors emerge those stable and predictable behavior components for the machinery of an increasingly impersonal, businesslike society. And since they're meant to find their place in mass society, they end up being widget Christians, pretty much indistinguishable from one another.

Many churches seek to take the gospel seriously, yet poorly resist the culture's demand that they produce practitioners of "Moralistic Therapeutic Deism,"[2] which is Christian Smith's term for a vaguely spiritual stance marked by a desire to feel good and at the same time be seen as a good person. The contradiction between the two desires is papered over by the assumption that desire need not be educated. Instead of churches that teach how difficult it is to educate desire, we tacitly assume—as moralistic therapeutic deists—that the culture's ranking of desire is largely legitimate. If it were otherwise, would every teen in the youth group, without question or discussion, have a smartphone? Granted, many churches provide seminars for youth on how to handle social media, but isn't this like allowing every child to have, say, a hungry panther in his or her bedroom and saying, "Here's a saddle; maybe you can figure out how to ride it"? And why *shouldn't* teens gravitate toward an attachment to devices, since they've been taking notes, since toddlerhood, on their own parents' attachment to the same devices?

---

2. Smith, *Soul Searching*, 162.

INTRODUCTION: THE BATTLE

On the other hand, churches with a less deistic and more legalistic bent tend to shame all desire. The simplistic way of saying this is "Don't want anything but God," heavily implying that God resents any aliveness we have that doesn't relate directly to him. A far better way to convey the same thought, but with vastly more nuance, is to teach Augustine's "You have made us for yourself, and our heart is restless until it rests in you."[3] Augustine (and behind him, Paul, Jesus, and the first commandment of the Decalogue) shows us that we must labor to set our loves in order (which opens the door to the education of desire). Instead, churches of this kind question the livingness of all desire. They wrongly take the profound words "Lord, to whom shall we go? You have words of eternal life" (John 6:68) and hone desire down to wanting *only* God, instead of following the Bible's emphasis on wanting God *first*. Many of the more legalistic might shudder to know that an early Christian theologian, Irenaeus, said, "For the glory of God is a living man."[4] The context of Irenaeus's words proves that he means much more than "a man who is alive." He means that as humans are redeemed in Christ and see the Father through the Son, they come fully alive. The *capacity* to desire is good. The direction and ordering of *specific* desires is meant to be transformed by the light of God's word.

How can Bible-teaching churches (let alone those more casual about proclaiming the biblical message) do a better job of making disciples? How might the tide of "*Christian* Moralistic Therapeutic Deism"[5] be made to recede in favor of a vigorous Christianity that not only enjoys the mouthfeel of such concepts as Trinity, sin, grace, heaven, hell, faith, Christ's return, atonement, the cross, resurrection, and Pentecost but also opens up their true nature in order to give the Holy Spirit more raw material for God's campaign to form us into "the image of His Son" (Rom 8:29)? Spiritual formation and feeling good do not *inherently* exclude one another, but they *are* often going to part ways if we're serious about discipleship. How serious are we?

---

3. Augustine, *Confessions*, 3.
4. Irenaeus, *Against Heresies*, bk. 4, ch. 20, para. 7.
5. Smith, *Soul Searching*, 171.

STUCK

Churches of a more legalistic bent *do* wrongly harbor a suspicion that feeling good is anti-God. "Deny yourself" all too often comes to mean "Don't have a self." How might we avoid this oversimplistic conclusion? And how might we avoid conveying the idea that pure self-loathing best proves one's devotion to God? The stakes can be high. I remember a young man in my counseling practice whose agony stemmed from the fact that he had spent his high school and college years trying not to want anything, so much so that, though he was a gifted violinist, he never picked up that instrument again after a youth pastor preached on wanting God so much that *no* secondary desire could be legitimate, forgetting that the last words of Matt 6:33 are "and all these things will be added to you." Did we lose the equivalent of an Itzak Perlman or even a Beethoven in the superficiality of this message? Wasn't this young man's profound agony cruelly unnecessary?

Given such questions, you might think you're about to launch into a tome about the social environment that surrounds the church and leaks secularity into it. That would be a great book I'm not qualified to write.[6] The book you're now reading explores another, related tension. It is that between the story our behavior indicates we're *actually* living out (one of self-development and feeling as good as *we* want to feel) and the story in which we *claim* to live (following Christ, *to* whom we give short shrift despite our strong protests to the contrary). It's the same tension as that between "Christian Moral Therapeutic Deism" and the call to be disciples of Christ. How do we get stuck in small stories of self-concern at the same time that we allege we are followers of the one who demonstrated a *lack* of self-concern? In other words, how do we get lost in the war between flesh and Spirit and end up too often and too long serving in the armies of the flesh? How, that is, do we become reverse born again in the sense that we move forward by faith into the kingdom of God yet are in reverse when it comes to sanctification? How is it that the church at large tends to overlook the chilling words "the mind set on the flesh is death" (Rom 8:6)?

---

6. Christian Smith's book, cited previously, would be a good place to start.

INTRODUCTION: THE BATTLE

Let me give you an example: me. After graduating from a well-regarded seminary, I became the pastor of a fledgling church. Times were busy getting the newly planted church off the ground. It was like a precocious toddler needing much and lurching around, getting into everything. I had my own issues, too. I feared failure and at the same time craved affirmation. I didn't know it at the time, but my internal conflict had roots in the fact that my father had divorced my mother when I was nineteen and had completely abandoned me and my brothers in the process. Deep within, I stored away a sad, subconscious question: "What kind of son can't even keep his dad around?" And the implied answer wasn't good: "A son who is uninspiring and easily tossed away." Basically, I felt that my dad looked at me on the way out the door and gave a shrug that said, "Meh." And never looked back.

That's the message that lodged itself deep in my innermost being. As it tolled out a hidden and deep doom in my heart, I grew to dread failure and to crave affirmation. My struggle was this: If your own father can throw you away, is there *any* security? Without knowing it, I'd determined that security would be grounded in my own performance, racking up enough successes to "prove" I was worth others' time and attention. I worked like John Henry against the steam drill, trying to amass enough "attaboys" to pour at the feet of my approval idol, a sort of latter-day Baal smiling on my disordered desire. Week after week, as I preached, the back of my mind churned with fear. "How is this going? What do they think? Will they come back next week?" My desire for approval outcompeted my desire for God, and my loves were badly out of order.

I developed a blindness, a caul over my eyes that only God could tear away. My desperate careening about for validation almost destroyed my marriage. Too often, I would leave early and come home late. I was like a coal miner who had to dig out a certain quota each day. Down in the mines, laboring for the payoffs of others' approval, I'd lose track of time, come home exhausted, throw my wife a bone or two of tucking the kids into bed, and then start over. What could she say? I was doing "the Lord's work." By the time a decade had passed, she was deeply depressed. I couldn't figure out what was wrong with her. When her waves of pain turned into thoughts of suicide, she landed, like a butterfly with ragged wings, in the office of a perceptive counselor. Through that gentleman's work, God tore the caul from my eyes, and I saw how driven, selfish, and afraid I had been. I discovered with a brutal shock that "the mind set on the flesh is death" (Rom 8:6). In this case, the suicidal thoughts of my wife signaled the probing force of death.

A battle had raged in my soul between blinded me and the me who longed to see. I'd been too harnessed in to notice. This book is about that same battle in every Christian, the one baldly described in Gal 5:17: "For the flesh lusts against the Spirit, and the Spirit [is] against the flesh, for these are in opposition to each other."

Full of beauty is a human relationship based on mutual, unconditional love. When that kind of relationship grows among Christians, it's a powerful source of knowledge: "By this all men will know that you are My disciples, if you have love for one another" (John 13:35). How does the world know that discipleship to Jesus is real? The fog is cleared by Christian love. But what is Christian love? It's love that progressively bears the marks of *agapé*, which means it's directed by a choice of the will, a choice to esteem the other and express goodwill regardless of the merit of the other. It's the love Christ exemplifies and the love at the center of John 3:16: "For God so loved the world." This is the love Christ has in mind when he says, "By this [kind of love for one another] all men will know that you are My disciples."

Given that (1) Christ calls believers to mutual *agapé*, and (2) answering that call gives the world knowledge of God's kingdom, it stands to reason that the forces of darkness would attack this model of relationships at every opportunity. In my decades of counseling practice, I've seen abundant evidence of this sustained, merciless attack. The attack is obvious when Christians are openly adversarial to one another. Much more subtle is the attack that lures Christians into arrangements with one another instead of relationships.

What do I mean by "arrangements"? The word "arrange" has a basic meaning: "to put in a row."[7] A connotation is "to regulate." When I say Christians too often end up in arrangements with one

---

7. *Webster's Third New International Dictionary* (1966), s.v. "arrange."

INTRODUCTION: THE BATTLE

another, I mean their interactions tend to be highly regulated, and that by some other energy than *agapé*. For that matter, *agapé* doesn't aim to regulate but to do good to the beloved. Its energy is too warm to regulate, desiring instead to pursue aims that may constructively deregulate one or both persons or parties.

What is the energy that generates arrangements instead of relationships? To put a point on it, it's the energy of the flesh. The flesh is humanity under the sign of sin, and sin's heart consists of the pride to dethrone God, the anxiety at having enthroned oneself, and sensuality enough to soothe the anxiety and give pride a fresh start. The flesh, our drive to sin, is the inflamed self, and the inflammation is caused by the impossible task of making life feel like "home" in an inhospitable world. Since its propensity is ever to curve back to self-concern, the flesh has no brief for anything like real relationships. Rather, its aim is to arrange people into categories such as (1) enemies to be neutralized, (2) resources to be used, (3) nobodies to be ignored, and (4) unclassifiables to be watched carefully.

Christians are too often mired in arrangements, and when they emerge from arrangements, they may well become adversarial ("Look what you did to me!"). This atmosphere, obviously, veers far from "by this all men will know that you are My disciples."

As is obvious from my own story, by the time most couples stand at the altar, they are already wounded by the selfishness of others (parents, friends, lovers, shattered dreams). Each houses an energy to survive, driven not by the pain of wounds per se but by the flesh's interpretation of that pain. The interpretation? Pain just means God doesn't care, you are on your own, and you must achieve safety and control in a harsh world. As couples vow to love, honor, and cherish one another, they have no awareness that such an antirelational energy is already holding them apart. Already moving more toward an arrangement than a relationship, marriages are hampered from the get-go.

This budding marital emergency is troubling (and, by extrapolation, the trouble applies to relationships in general). Two seemingly well-intended people are poised, even at the altar, to do great damage to one another because each is already stuck in a story

STUCK

of self-driven survival. How do we get stuck in our stories? How do we arrive at key points in our lives with so little awareness of where we really are? Recently, at a church leaders' retreat, the pastor underlined the value of "meeting people where they are." I immediately wrote in the margin of my handout, "What if people don't know where they are?" Later, when I posed this question to him, he showed little interest in grappling with its implications. But I'm not picking on him, because in my lifetime in church environments of one sort and another, I've seldom found the church ready to go where people really are. Why might this be true? My sense of it is that in our flesh-driven comfort zones, we simply don't want to be in over our heads with other people. And the truth is that if we find out where we and where others really are, we'll be in over our heads.

CHAPTER 1
Conundrum

The pain that can maul our lives is a force that blinds us. I witness this often in my counseling practice. Recently, my first counselee of the day told me this story: A car wreck three years ago shattered his body. His left arm remains 80 percent paralyzed; his left leg, 20 percent. Reconstructive surgery on his broken neck left him in excruciating pain. A prescribed opioid pill and a morphine patch partly control the agony. He tried to go back to work but says he can't pass a drug test because of the medications. His requests for doctors' notes to validate his needs for the pain relievers get lost in bureaucracy.

Now he's self-employed. Sometimes, that goes all right; other times, the physical pain straps him to his bed. He did manage to finish a significant job a few months ago, but the general contractor went belly up and can't pay him. Futility tracks him like a great cat. Why, he asks, did he go through the miracle of walking again only to wonder why he survived? What's the point "if I can't contribute to my family financially?" Probing further, I find his wife isn't, in his opinion, very supportive. And a year ago, he endured the shock of finding his best friend dead of a self-inflicted gunshot wound. He has never known his father, who abandoned him when he was three. He wonders, "When do the locusts come?"

The pain is so great that he can't see its potential. It drives him and blinds him, as can happen to any of us. In its intensity, it races around him like a relentless border collie, keeping him in a circle of despair.

I often show up in the middle of a story that could go either way. I'm referring to my counseling practice—but any "people helper" could say the same—where I find myself with strugglers who are each besieged by a disappointing story. That's hard enough, but on top of that, the story has developed its own reinforcing themes, its own payoffs. A payoff is any personal advantage, obvious or hidden, that comes through the way one lives within that disappointing story. Since our motivations aren't always clear to us, payoffs are often not obvious, pulling us along without our knowing it. Since this is so, it can be hard to resist our stories' power to drive us. We become unwitting compulsives.

For example, I work with another man who cannot give his wife any space. Afraid she won't be faithful to him, he crowds her, calls her all day, shows up by surprise to see whether she is where she claims she'll be, demands a constant accounting of her time, and so on. His marriage is going to ruin. So, what's the payoff for him? He is determined never to be surprised, never to be caught off guard. And, sure enough, he is accomplishing that goal. The goal is so enticing that breaking out of his old story (where unfaithfulness is always impending) involves a terrible struggle to enter a new story of trust and vulnerability. *That* story would destroy the protective payoff of the old story, because trust and vulnerability, by definition, include the possibility of the unexpected, the surprising.

But it turns out that in a previous marriage, his first wife cheated on him multiple times. Traumatized by the pain of broken trust, he's blind to his impact on his current marriage.

These self-protective stories, then, are amazingly strong and convincing to the folks I join along the way, just as mine was in my years as a pastor. I see myself in others as I look back to my early years of marriage. It took ten years and some powerful intervention to reveal my destructive impact. My wife's depression had been announcing it, but I was as deaf as I was blind. Her cries had gone unnoticed, like billboards on an interstate. The durability of our survival stories is striking: we cling to them like barnacles to a piling. Or do the stories cling to *us*? Or both? One friend who read this paragraph asked me, "Are you asking us to divorce from our stories? Or just integrate them into a bigger story of Christ?" My response is that we should *not* divorce ourselves from our survival stories. Rather, we should seek to understand them. Further, we can't integrate them into Christ's story until we *know* them.

Before we apply the wisdom of Christ's story, then, we should look at our own life's story as if through bifocals. Through one half of the lens, we see our biography. This biographical aspect of our story is captured in events, people, and documents (like birthdays, birth certificates, family reunions, social security cards, school events, deeds to homes and properties, rental agreements, getting married, emails, our online life, etc.). This biographical view records our life as a series of occurrences. It's full of anecdotes and documents, but it isn't tied together; it isn't a story.

Then there is the other lens, what I'd call the theological lens. Through it, we find that meanings often hide within this seemingly simple march of thing after thing. The meanings are there, but they tend to be submerged because they're often painful. They can be painful because we are designed for a nobler world, a world that fits us far better than this fallen one. Since we don't live in that world, we tend to "suppress the truth in unrighteousness" (Rom 1:18), including the truth that the broken, groaning world in which we live can never offer enough fulfillment to repair the wound of our losing Eden. Theologically speaking, this wound can neither be avoided nor healed through our own efforts. But our biography can *look* as if there's no wound at all.

Here, for example, is a bare occurrence, a piece of biography. The parents of an eight-year-old boy walk into his bedroom one night. They announce that they will no longer read stories and snuggle with the young boy at bedtime. They tell him he is old enough to move beyond these rituals. Time to grow up! They then turn and leave. For the parents, a policy decision has been issued. That's the end of it.

That's the bare occurrence, but there's much more: the meaningful story is that the boy has come deeply to enjoy these times of nurture, conversation, and creativity. When his parents announce the dawn of a colder era, the boy feels abandoned and confused. He

STUCK

feels foolish, too, for assuming these delightful times of relational reassurance would continue. "Stupid me," he thinks. "I was an idiot for delighting in being tucked in and read to. Shouldn't have needed so deeply this goodness and love. I can't be a sissy like that. I'm on my own now." Most of this is below the level of consciousness. Again, we "suppress the truth in unrighteousness." The suppressed pain begins to weave itself into a story where the payoff consists of proving to himself that he needs nothing. Imagine what that story will do to his marriage years later. And to his parenting.

Through his cold style of relating (so devastating to his wife and children), the man was telling, all unknown to him or them, the story of his abandoned heart. The cold relational code through which the story was told concealed his loss, locked up his heart, distanced him from the scary love that had failed him in yesteryear. He marched through life and became a successful physician, and he *looked* fine. The biographical sketch of his life left a good impression.

As we move beyond his personal biography (the list of life events), we glimpse that theology underlines the heart's flirtation with transcendence, with hope, with God. Theology is the heart daring, yet fearing, to believe in happiness again. Children are created for a world where parents don't parent through bare statements of policy. Children are looking for a story tuned to a heart made to be loved, not managed; made for knowing and being known. We are not to divorce ourselves from our stories, as my friend's question implied. Rather, we are to *enter* them and learn their meanings. We are to tease apart our violated longings *and* our own sinful ways of protecting ourselves from further violation, thinking and praying deeply about both. We're to learn that we have cooked up a story of survival too small for a heart designed for love, which is to say a heart deeply influenced by the fact that we are made in God's image.

It takes guts to enter our deeper stories. Who wants to see the shattered transcendence littering the floor of one's heart? And who wants to see one's sinful attempts to glue transcendence back together with the childish pastepots of self-sufficiency? It's easier to hide in the self-deceit that biography *is* the story, that bare occurrence is all there is. *That's* the too-limited story line from which we *do* need to divorce ourselves. We should not separate from our *stories* but from our turning those stories into one-thing-after-another with little to color them with meaning. Our biographies are not just filled with discrete events but with a task. The task consists of understanding the events as meaningful and as calling to one another for a narrative thread. The task includes seeing the sense in them by looking at them from the vantage point of an overarching story, a story from beyond us.

The story that opens this chapter helps in the task because it refuses the enticements of mere biography. It's too powerful to be boiled down to "stuff happens." It comes across with a wallop, calling for some humility in the listener. How do I respond to such an overwhelming story, especially when I'm not in his shoes? A man has been hounded into a corner. It's dark. The enemy is at him (the enemy of financial ruin or paralyzing depression, probably both). He's telling a story I'm not sure I could handle myself. I certainly shouldn't say, "Those are bare occurrences; just live with them. Stuff happens." But what *do* I say? Are there any options here other than withdrawal or facile advice?

Yes. A crucial point is to ask oneself: Am I reduced to my situation, or am I willing and able to see an alternative? Alternatives can begin when *we refuse to let disappointing things become the defining things*. This refusal is a weapon against despair, a way of finding leverage amid overwhelming adversity. It's Sam reminding Frodo of the Shire as his friend loses hope on the slopes of Mount Doom. It's God on another mountain reinflating Elijah with hope through his still, small voice. Either it's the case that the bleak situation is all-encompassing, or it's the case that important realities are *still free* from it. If that is true, then *we're* free to find definitions for our lives other than the defining power of heavy disappointments. But the disappointing story doesn't give up easily; it threatens to drown the alternatives (and us) in sheer pain. It threatens to be the ruler of all other stories. It threatens to destroy hope; it threatens to de-story hope. And when that happens, we get stuck in our smaller stories.

"Where was God when I was sexually abused all that time?" she asked me. Rather than launch a defense of God (as I might have not too many years ago), I was enabled by grace to hear her question as a struggle with suffocation. She felt suffocated by the

STUCK

excruciating pain in a story where she'd been turned into a degraded object for years. Was it just one brutal event after another? On one hand, it was that. On the other, can a big-enough story be found to contain the abuse tale and infuse it with meaning? And do so while avoiding the trap of tossing platitudes at her from a safe distance? Or minimizing her pain?

Where do we run when crushed by disappointments? Where do we turn when the disappointments command us to despair? "Curse God and die!" said Job's wife, and her relatives are legion. Is there an alternative to such futility? What do we do when we hit that final, fatal wall where it is written, "All your dreams are over, and you were a fool to trust in them"? Do we just give up?

I'd say that's good counsel: give up. Before you go out and try that advice, though, pay careful attention to *what it's wise to give up on*. My invitation is that we give up on the ways we've been trying painfully and foolishly to make life work. That is, *stop surviving*. Okay, I'll grant you: that's a conversation stopper. "Stop surviving" sounds an awful lot like "Stop breathing." Sometimes, though, a perspective becomes inviting through how paradoxical it is. "Stop surviving" seems a fool's maxim at first. Inside us, there's an incredulous resistance that says, "I *will* survive, and no one has the right to say anything against it." While this response has many layers, one of them is the voice of Western culture in the past two to three hundred years. This voice is another version of Job's wife—only, this time, instead of "Curse God and die," the voice says, "Ditch God and do it your way." About this voice of self-sufficiency, Gerrit Dawson, in his wonderful book *Jesus Ascended*, says, "We live and work amidst a very loud, insistent story. The culture tells us insistently that we are individuals whose decisions belong to the individual alone. It is up to each of us to pursue our happiness in ways we choose . . . ."[1] We who live in the West (basically, Europe, the United States, and Canada) exist in a matrix of teachings and ideas that center on affirming human autonomy. The last five hundred years of Western culture are like a powerful generator that has produced a mix of self-reliance and machine efficiency. Be your unique self, do

---

1. Dawson, *Jesus Ascended*, 25.

CONUNDRUM

your thing, find your dream, boost your self-esteem—these are the voices that create a dominant-cultural swirl that engulfs us.[2] Like fish, we don't even know we're wet. This giant of cultural command weighs on our hearts, proposing strongly that our survival tools are justified beyond all question. That is, if it helps us survive on our own terms, then it's good, and it's justified. So, when someone suggests that we stop surviving, we look at her as if she had said, "Drink the ocean."

Our programmed hearts must rise out of this valorizing of self-sufficiency. Yet, it is the very air our hearts breathe. How *does* one learn to stand away from his/her mental universe? This is our conundrum.

The fact that this point of view is *Western*, however, should give us pause. After all, it's a *culturally driven point of view*. As such, it has no automatic authority. For all we know, it has no more authority than the now-fading cultural practice of suttee (widow burning) in India. Two questions come to mind: First, since this Western self-sufficiency is, now we see, open to scrutiny, where do we go for a vantage point to discern whether it has any authentic truth value? Second, could it be the case that the culture's call to survive morphs into a lonely self-sufficiency that cuts us off from rich resources? How much of the power of our old stories comes from our being bogged down in a cultural lie? Is there a fulcrum we could find to help us leverage ourselves out of our old stories?

2. Trueman, *Modern Self*, 46.

CHAPTER 2
Fulcrum

An old story: several blind men, upon examining an elephant, are each asked what he thought he had hold of. One, gripping the tail, answers, "A snake." Another answers, "A tree," having grasped a leg. The point is clear: without their sight, the blind men have no hope of overcoming their limited vantage points. In the same way, Western culture commends self-sufficiency without having a big-picture vantage point from which to make such a sweeping ethical move. How can there be a vantage point when immanence is all there is? Given that the secular worldview has little or no room for transcendence, it must, by definition, have little or no room for a vantage point outside itself. For all the secularists know, boosting a culture of self-sufficiency is tantamount to mistaking the tail for the whole elephant.

Where *do* we go for a vantage point? Unless we can back up and see the "elephant," how can we escape the limits of shortsightedness? From where, then, will a greater sight line become possible? My short answer is "from the house of memory." Meaning what? The house of memory is an image that emerges from Isa 51:1–3: "Listen to me, you who pursue righteousness, / you who seek the Lord: / look to the rock from which you were hewn, / and to the quarry from which you were dug. / Look to Abraham your father / and to Sarah who bore you in pain." If a metaphor contains a story, what is the story here? Clearly, the author gives us a metaphor based on quarrying rock. The metaphor becomes a way to talk about both memory and security. The verses speak of a couple of "parent rocks," Abraham and Sarah. They are, in some sense, the source and foundation of those "who pursue righteousness." Something about them leads to a sense of security. Isaiah invites us to dig deeply into their examples.

But Abraham and Sarah can't act as founding sources unless we *remember* them. "Look to" them, says the Scripture—that is, remember them. Why? Because they struggle through their own faithlessness and emerge as those who radically trust God. God finally draws them to his heart. Abraham, for example, shows what it is to wait on God in faith, especially his stunning faith in laying his son, Isaac, on an altar. Here is a radical surrender to which God responds by providing a substitute, introducing the whole theme of one who lovingly takes the place of another. What of Sarah? She gives birth, says the Scripture, in pain. What is her pain? Not the obvious pain of childbirth; that would be unremarkable—one would *assume* that childbirth would hurt physically. Sarah's pain in childbirth is that she had to wait helplessly for *God's* time to come for childbearing. She had to take a back seat and watch Hagar get the glory of fulfilling her husband's dream of having a child. Only after deep humiliation was she able to see God do the impossible: she became pregnant in her extreme old age. Only after extended loss does Sarah receive the happiness of fulfillment.

Scripture, then, jump-starts our memory after it has been buried under withering piles of discouragement. Discouragement tempts us to forget, but Scripture is like a sprawling house full of redemptive memories; and those who "pursue righteousness" are invited not merely to tour it occasionally but to *live* there. Scripture is the *house* of memory, and a house is not a house when we only visit it from time to time. It becomes a house when it is a dwelling. When we live there, we live among founding memories.

Two things are crucial here. First, a founding memory gives us a place to stand. It reminds us that in spite of chaos, there is an underlying story that issues from God's nature. We stand on the foundation of his character and in the circle of his promises. We refuse to seek other founding memories or messages, because we trust that God's story provides the surplus of meaning that

STUCK

un-smothers us from despair's coils. Second, living in "the house of memory" expands our recall far beyond remembering our own past; we can now remember *God's past with his people*. This past becomes *our* past, *our* memory. Our memory becomes *huge*, maybe huge enough to help us counter despair. Through these founding memories, we live among stories. We live among remembrances, and we are secured as we internalize them. Our used-up hearts often become like dried and discarded tea bags; but they rehydrate as we soak, immersed in fresh water: the stories of God's past with God's people.

There is a story in the house of memory about a man with his back quite literally to the wall (like the man with his back to the wall in the opening story of the previous chapter). The story in the house of memory occupies Ps 57. There, David is holed up in a cave with a few loyal men. After running for his life for weeks, he's now hiding, but his refuge could easily become a death trap. The "title" of the psalm declares David's tension: "An epigram[1] of David, when he fled from Saul, in the cave."

What does the man in the cave say? He begins:

> I will cry to God Most High,
> To God who accomplishes all things for me.
> He will send from heaven and save me;
> He reproaches him who tramples upon me.
> God will send forth His lovingkindness and His truth.

How is David able to flee into a cave, all harassed and hunted, and yet, in hope, call out to God as shelter? Why doesn't the psalm begin with "Poor me; I deserve a pity party; no one understands me; life stinks"? How was David able to rise above such an attitude? After all, he had been successful, followed God, served Saul, been admired—what did he get for these things? He became the target of Saul's paranoia and ended up a fugitive.

How has David come to live in a story that overcomes his fear of Saul? How is he able to move from anxiety to security? Why is

---

1. The Hebrew word translated as "epigram" can mean "inscription," "epigram," or possibly, "secret prayer" (Koehler et al., *Hebrew and Aramaic Lexicon*, 582–83).

this shift relatively rare in my counseling experience? Heck, why is it so hard for *me* to make this shift? What would need to happen to help us make it?

For starters, we need to delve into the key words in this psalm (after all, stories are built of words). We discover, when we do, that even bare words can invite us toward alternative stories. Stories of rescue and deliverance lie behind and among words like "shelter," "shadow," "destruction," "refuge" (all from Ps 57). These muscular words call us to the house of memory, there to retrieve stories where the Deliverer has come, stories where the uncertainty has passed and the happy ending has been decisively accomplished. They call us to see a Lazarus coming out of the grave, gaping at new life. We realize we don't just live in the confinements of our personal story as if it's locked in amber. Instead, we live in a gathering of stories, a storied land where an assembly of expansive narratives comes alongside the wounds, sin, and loneliness of our confined stories to unfold other versions of life. They arrive like great physicians, calling us to newness and wellbeing. The stories are like loving parents calling to us when we're lost, calling us home.

The house of memory with its many God-given stories deconstructs the American story of the isolated self with its own private rules for conducting life and relationships. When we scrutinize the Western story of self-sufficiency, we see a story that has no story*teller*. It has no authority, because it has no author. It cannot be a resource, because it has no source. This false story is strong not because it has an author but because it helps us whistle past the graveyard of meaninglessness. It means something merely because it helps us to not mean nothing. This thought leads us back to the enduring power of our biographical stories, even though they are meaning-starved, even when they lead to hopelessness. For example, one can pursue the hope of being desired, and pursue it so intensely that he or she betrays all other values just to gain someone, anyone who makes one feel desired. The pain of discarding many important values (a marriage, children) to gain that one payoff—"I am a desired man or woman"—often fails to offset the sheer gratification that a thirsty soul feels upon being wanted. This trade-off amounts to one's gaining the world yet losing one's soul, and Jesus soberly warns us against it. Yet the temporary satisfaction of an agonizing thirst can blind us to all else.

Too often, then, we hold tightly to our stories not because they are true but because they confer a benefit we deem life-giving. If a story *feels* as though it gives life, then it must be good. Who cares about whether it does justice to what is true? Many of our stories work for us in the short run simply as powerful sources of good feelings. In the long run, though, they destroy us; because they veer off from what's true.

N. T. Wright writes about the relationship between the world in which we live and the stories we tell. He picks up on this theme of falsehood in our stories:

> Humans live in overlapping worlds, and, as individuals or as groups, they may well tell themselves different and overlapping, but also competing, stories. In addition, the stories that are explicitly told by a group or individual may well be consciously or unconsciously deceitful, and will require checking in the light of actual praxis and of a wider symbolic universe. What someone habitually *does*, and the symbols around which they order their lives, are at least as reliable an index to their worldview as the stories they "officially" tell.[2]

In other words, sometimes we tell one story (I value this; I value that), but our behavior tells another story (I value this by my spoken words, but I rarely support that value by what I do).

For example, a woman *says* she wants counseling, wants to get help with her marriage. What she actually *does* is fight the process, constantly justify herself, act seductive, construe events so as to be easily offended, and cancel the last appointment half an hour ahead of time. Then she resents how the practice is structured, gets angry about being charged for a missed appointment, and never comes back. She drives a red, late-model convertible (*symbolic* of her mid-forties preoccupation with youth and beauty and her insecurities about growing older). Some part of her wants a new story, but

---

2. Wright, *People of God*, 40–41.

something more powerful is blocking her own stated goal. Again, why does the old story have such controlling power?

First, the old story is *familiar*. It gives us permission to avoid the challenge of newness. And by saving us from newness, the old story, second, provides some sense of *control*. Third, it saves us from *risk*. Fourth, sometimes (always?) the old story is a defense against *shame*; i.e., it hides shame or answers shame's accusations. Fifth, the old story may allay some key *fears*, because it prepares us to be *ready*. Spring-loaded with tried-and-true responses, we're ready for whatever comes. Readiness may include *fight, flight, or freeze* responses that provide a sense of immediate control. Sixth, the old story goes a long way toward providing an *identity*. The story settles us into a familiar version of ourselves, and that familiarity brings predictability and stability. A *new* story calls on us to soften our identity, to make it more changeable, to experiment with another version of ourselves. This can be unsettling, and we deeply need Christ to see us through the challenges of newness.

The next answers as to why our old stories remain powerful are a bit more lengthy.

Seventh, Wright discusses a current view of reading texts (any text) that is quite private: "There is only my reading, your reading and an infinite number of other possible readings."[3] I wonder whether in Western culture we've become so deeply, subliminally trained to over-respect the particularity and assumed validity of every story that it's less and less possible to subvert any story by any other. "Well, that's how you read life; I don't. Your truth is your truth, and my truth is mine." If that is everyone's final answer, why even offer an alternative story? If the story my flesh is telling about how I should live life seems valid to me, who is to say otherwise?

Eighth, there's the vast and massive flow of punditry in every American TV room (let alone through radio, the multiform internet, the surviving newspapers and newsmagazines). The sheer word vomit floods into the psyche of the citizenry to the saturation point. Ad nauseam, ad infinitum, the "beat goes on"—the interpretive commentary surges around and over everything as commentator

---

3. Wright, *People of God*, 66.

STUCK

after commentator tells the "real" story of what's going on: Here's what the Democrats are really doing. Here's the Republican agenda (you can't see it, but I can). Here's what the president/Congress/the media are up to, here's what the economy will do, here's why crime is up, down, statistically flat. Etc., etc. Could it be that this semiofficial storytelling in its sheer volume creates a need for folks to hunker down deeper into their own stories simply to survive? Does information overload tempt us reflexively to fortify ourselves behind our familiarly storied identities, as if to say that at least *something* is stable? Do we become like the anorexic who thinks, "At least I can control *this*" (food intake), since she feels out of control everywhere else? That is, do we clutch our stories to ourselves in a bid for control because we are jostled by media-sponsored narratives of life that, by their sheer volume, loosen our hold on our own stories? The difference between this jostling mob of stories and the gathering of stories in the house of memory is profound. The first results in insecure, unfounded stories that numb our anxieties without resolving them. The second results in grounded stories, those based in the call of a transcendent author. They are faithful to reality. As such, they invite our old stories to new possibilities. They help us face our anxieties and resolve them.

Ninth, yet another source of the power of old, confining stories could be the American value of self-reliance and self-determination. When one tries to subvert an old story, maybe resistance kicks in at least in part owing to the "Don't tread on me" norm that is deeply held in our culture. "No one is going to tell me what to do!" How many times have I heard that (and felt that in myself)? Our culture, then, plays its part in setting up a built-in tension between any two parties when one is seeking to influence the other. Maybe in our culture, any source of influence raises the issue of authority—i.e., "What right have you to mess around with my story?" It's as if our self-developed stories have a greater sovereignty than God himself. We allow them to rule us. We submit to their power to define us more than we open up to God's new defining of us through Christ.

Take Christian radio, for example. Why does nearly every radio ministry (with a few exceptions) offer a teacher or preacher whose persona has it all together? As a friend of mine observed,

FULCRUM

it's as if all these ministries exude the following attitude: "If, in the very deep past, I ever struggled, *now* I've got it figured out." Few convey the humility to reveal *current* struggle—to admit that they still need (present tense) God's work *right now and every day* to help them clarify where they are in the battle between stories. Why the apparent pressure to convey that the Christian story is about a finished product, giving the impression that we've arrived? Can it be that much of Christianity has come under the influence of the American story of self-mastery? I am not, of course, suggesting that Christ is not at the center of these ministries. My point is that Christ's centrality may be clouded over by the powerful interplay of personal and cultural narratives that, in spite of our Lord's influence, still have the strength to steer a ministry (or an individual) toward a value (self-mastery) that Christ himself would lead believers to reject.

Given these nine possible reasons for the power of our old stories, spiritual formation should include an invitation to explore our dominant stories, their sources, and their functions. I'd go so far as to say that discipleship *without* the exploring of personal stories sets us up for failure. But is this emphasis on stories supported by the biblical worldview? I think so, even though, yes, one can't find a proof text that says, "Thou shalt include the analysis of personal stories in your approach to discipleship." Be that as it may, a bigger picture of Scripture would have to include "the call of stories."[4] After all, the Bible is written as a vast story that contains hundreds of smaller stories. Narratives inhabit narratives that inhabit the narrative, so that the Bible is a vast tissue of storytelling. How different it would be if the Bible were composed of mathematical formulae or bare lists of rules!

The Bible's focus on the story genre makes me think of psychotherapist Hans Strupp's *Psychotherapy in a New Key*. He distinguishes between content and process (roughly, content is what gets conveyed verbally and nonverbally between parties; process involves *how and why* it is conveyed).[5] Strupp uses the term "interpersonal

---

4. Coles, *Call of Stories*, cover jacket.
5. Strupp and Binder, *Psychotherapy*, 102–3.

scenario" to delve deeper into the idea of process. "Interpersonal scenario" describes what the client is seeking to "enact" between him- or herself and the therapist.[6] The idea of enactment means that drama is a fundamental genre of human interaction. That is, it's not just that the counselee is telling a story but that he or she is pulling the therapist into a role in the story. The therapist is cast in a certain way, and things can get sticky when the therapist departs from that role. On the other hand, the therapist *must* depart from the role or she won't be able to help. The therapist cannot passively *be* the counselee's fantasy companion. Nor can she unthinkingly assume *any* role into which the counselee seeks to cast him or her. The therapist must step back and work to see the story (the drama) in which the counselee (and now the therapist) is embroiled. Janet Malcolm puts it this way: "We must grope around for each other through a dense thicket of absent others."[7] Not only is there a hard-to-discern story going on, there are also invisible but powerful characters populating (and often interfering with) the interaction.

Wouldn't this "thicket of absent others" (who are actually quietly, powerfully present) also be present between a human and God? Most certainly. The most influential absent yet present other between ourselves and God is Satan. Consider: the first move Satan makes in Scripture is to distort Eve's picture of God. In his serpentine form, he says to her, "You surely shall not die [if you eat the forbidden fruit]. For God knows that in the day you eat from it your eyes will be opened, and you will be like God, knowing good and evil" (Gen 3:4–5). Here is a story indeed. It's a stunning exposé of the post-fall reality with which we have to contend. We now live in a story where an adversary seeks to distort our view of God. We are never free from the contention that God has withheld important facts, that God isn't entirely honest. Now our relationship with God is shot through with suspicion. If we live as if we're innocent of this suspicion, we fall into Satan's snare. His cloud is between us and our true Creator.

---

6. Strupp and Binder, *Psychotherapy*, 103.
7. Malcolm, *Psychoanalysis*, 6.

FULCRUM

This cloud ensures that more "absent others" will come between us and God. The most common one is our own earthly father. It has become a commonplace that our view of God is influenced heavily by our journey with our fathers. As soon as we say, "Our Father who art in heaven," we face the overlay of our father "who art in" our own homes and hearts (for better or worse) as we grew up. And if he wasn't there at all, he is apt to be very powerful indeed as a distortion of our picture of God.

Now, if the absent others are there, so are *their* stories. And their stories interact with ours such that another story (*about* that interaction) is formed. Multiple layers of stories influence our lives. We live in narrative strata that call for sorting and clarification. Given the centrality of stories, both in Scripture and in our lives, why have we missed "the call of stories" that is so obviously *there* in the Bible?

Here, we reach back for a question we asked some pages back: Could it be that the call to survive in a lonely self-sufficiency cuts us off from rich resources that are simply unavailable when we live on our islands of self-sufficiency? Survival is a bedfellow to loneliness. So, why do we settle for mere survival when it's so lonely? Why, in other words, are we so afraid to explore that call of stories? A possible answer is that most of us have significant struggles over the issues of hope and trust. That is, if I let you cross over to my island, I fear becoming vulnerable to you. If I allow you to hear my story, how can I trust that you'll respond empathetically, without a hidden agenda? At least I currently *have* a story. If I allow *you* inside that story, maybe you'll subvert it; and then what will I have left? How can I know that an alternate story you (or the Bible, or God) might propose isn't going to fail me? And if it fails me, then what? Can I really then go back to my old story? Or will I find myself in limbo? Will my last state be worse than my first (see Matt 12:45)?

There is a conflict in all of us, a conflict about the hope that there's a better story and another self that can be liberated, that can be found within the prison of paralysis, like a noble statue locked within a block of stone. The conflict about hope is unavoidable, for, given the conditions of a fallen world, that option for newness is often mocked, disappointed, buried alive, scorched, turned into a

STUCK

weapon against us. And often, these acts are carried out viciously by the self against the self. "Don't you dare come alive to hope!" the heart says to itself. "You fool! You might as well beg to be hurt." The sneer and snarl of such inner policing terrifies the hoping heart into shame and retreat.

And why, we think, *should* we get our hopes up? We've braved that before and been burned. Hope is vulnerable, and the whole point of our old story is to protect us from vulnerability. So, we fear invitations to vulnerability with their possibility of pain. No thanks. Inside ourselves, we might even find an intense rage at this invitation. It's the rage that furiously warns, "Keep away from my style of staying in control. You'd be going for my jugular. I won't allow it. I'll go for yours first." The Bible is a radical invitation to a new story, and there's a part of us that fears and hates it.

Our old stories, then, function to muffle disappointment—that which we've already had and that which we're still trying to avoid. Here's an example: in a recent counseling session, three members of a family are together, a son and his parents. The son tells a story. We step into that story together. It takes place during a Christmas season when the son is about thirteen. Holidays and special days are difficult for this family, because there's so much toxicity in their relationships that the atmosphere of a "special day" feels like a major pretense. The son (the youngest of four children) is especially turned off by such days. On this Christmas Day, something toxic happens at mealtime, some sarcastic sally from one family member to another. In response, the son leaves the table, goes to a nearby countertop, takes a large knife, and begins stabbing the counter and chipping it. His anger takes this form as if to say, "I myself have tried to be as hard as this countertop, but the blade of what happens in our family still cuts me to pieces." In his heart, he is disappointed severally: with his family for being so unsafe, with his parents for not restraining his siblings' verbal attacks on him, with life for being such a sad story, and most of all, with himself for not becoming hard enough to endure the pain. The story developing inside him is that he is the crazy one—he is the disappointment, the bad child, the one too crippled to "get" how to live above the pain. He is the social oddball who deserves to be rejected. He is the scapegoat. In these negative self-descriptions, all the disappointment in his story makes sense: if he were more competent at life, none of these bad things would happen; or if some of them did happen, they wouldn't hurt. Maybe, then, it's not that life is disappointing but that *he* is; and maybe, then, someday he can figure out how not to be. A pale hope remains. But such a wan and painful hope! How costly!

Like David, this young man waits in the cave "until destruction passes by" (Ps 57:1), but in this case, the cave is that of his own self-protection; and the destruction *doesn't* pass by. It keeps happening. It is relentless. It's as though Saul's killer squad bursts into the cave and kills David and all his men over and over. Why won't the pain stop? Doesn't this recurring nightmare mean the old story is king? Why hope for a new one when a new one never comes?

But wait. We're learning about these events in a counseling session where, for the first time, the son is able to talk about these sorrows to his parents. And they are hearing him without defensiveness. They are inviting him to talk these things through with them. And he is venturing to respond honestly. Newness may be in the offing. For the first time, his father is able to say to him, "You felt like the really evil one," and to say it with a tone of deep sorrow. Sometimes, newness starts in grief.

CHAPTER 3

Momentum

Seeing these newborn possibilities after so many years in the wilds of disappointment makes me ask: Are there places in the house of memory that reflect this same pattern of extended loss followed by hope? I think of Isa 5 and Isa 27, because both chapters focus on a story, the story of Israel as God's vineyard. Of course, Israel is not really a vineyard, and we know we're encountering a figure of speech, a metaphor. Again, every metaphor can be thought of as a miniature story. We might think, for example, "Israel is a vineyard? Well, how is that the case? How does Israel, in some ways, resemble cultivated grapevines? A vineyard to whom? Maybe there's a story here."

And so there is. In Isa 5, God calls the reader to witness a tragedy: the vineyard (Israel) on which God had focused love, time, and effort had done him the disservice of bearing worthless grapes. Anyone who has slaved over a garden only to have drought or pests or flood defeat all efforts so that the yield is nil will understand the anguish of Isa 5. But here is where the metaphor gets interesting. It's bad enough that a garden or an orchard would produce only the fruit of disappointment, but try extending that pain to a long-pursued, long-cherished relationship. It was a relationship, say, that began in high hopes on the part of a wooer who, with herculean strivings and sacrificial commitment, pursued his beloved. His message to her was, "You are made for a great love story, and I intend to protect you and preserve you so that you can have all of it." What answer did the beloved make? Gratefulness? Anticipation?

MOMENTUM

Commitment? Hardly. The answer was, "I will spread my legs to any passerby who will have me." Shocking? Yes, but these are the actual words of Scripture as God expresses his broken, betrayed heart (see Ezek 16:25). Now, what if *you* were the pursuing wooer catching your beloved right in the act of betraying you? Caught him or her in your own bed with another? Can you imagine how God feels? He wants you to. Why? So you know his heart.

The vineyard narrative, then, is one more attempt on God's part to tell how he feels. He says, in effect:

> You farmers out there. You know what it's like when your labor, care, and attention are rewarded with bitterness and loss. You've had the heavy, broken heart when massive sacrifice turns into terrible futility. Maybe you can weep with me, the one who, over and over again, pursued my people with passion and promise only to find them so hardened to me that they mocked me by their adulteries. I am a cuckolded husband.

God tells a story, a farmer's story dense with disappointment. He tells that story to convey a husband's story of betrayal. Why? To reveal God's heart as a place where disappointment strikes deeply, just as it does in ours. There are few anguishes like that of the crop failure that means no food, no money, no health; that means failure, anxiety, grief. Why would God pick this kind of anguish to reveal his own? He is telling us, "I am a stricken God." Why does he reveal this intimacy to us? Because God, too, has a story. To know God's heart is to know that God has a story, just as you have one.

God's story in the Old Testament often highlights his anguish. The stereotypical picture of the "Old Testament God" gives the impression of over-the-top divine anger. Walter Brueggemann says somewhere that God's anger is the flip side of his anguish.[1] God *does* get angry in the Old Testament (just as Jesus gets angry in the New Testament), but that anger is neither a fit of pique nor a bad mood looking for a target. God doesn't have an impulse to anger such that he's looking to discharge it. Rather, he has an impulse to restore creation, and when it resists this good and right intent,

---

1. Brueggemann, *Finally Comes*, 21.

STUCK

God experiences the disappointment expressed in Isa 5. And, yes, sometimes that anguish turns into anger as God seeks to draw the attention of Israel away from her lovers. Rather than read about his anger and interpret God as ill-tempered, we should move toward a story of a brokenhearted but determined pursuer.

Part of God's anger, too, issues from his hope. A friend asked me, "How can an omniscient being have hope? Doesn't the existence of hope imply an unknown outcome?" Short answer: Have you ever seen a dramatic scene in a movie a second time and, knowing the outcome, you still got caught up in the action, the passion, the tension? My point is that we can know what is going to happen and still be deeply affected by events leading up to the known outcome. I can't say how an omniscient being feels except by what that being reveals; and God reveals great passion, especially in those passages in the Prophets where he engages Israel furiously about known outcomes.

God knows the plans he has for his people. He can see what they cannot. He desires that they trust him by following and doing his will, which is for *shalōm*—that is, well-being, wholeness, salvation. When God's people *don't* trust, don't follow, don't worship, he sees the consequences of their choices and grieves. Isaiah 5 is an expression of that grief. Somehow, God's already knowing their future behavior does little to mitigate his passion. Again, that grief can become anger as God determines to call his people to repentance—that is, to returning to his ways of *shalōm*. If the proverb "Hope deferred makes the heart sick" (Prov 3:12) can be said of humans, perhaps it applies to God as well. Often, an angry person will explain his anger by saying, "I am sick of this." Sometimes, anger is heartsickness trying to rattle the cage of the foolish other. But why rattle the cage? In hope. That is, hope that the other might be jarred out of the rut of foolishness.

If Isa 5 darkens hope, in Isa 27, another vineyard passage, God's hope shines out. This time, the outcome radiates hope and joy. The passage begins in verses 2–3 with the following: "In that day [after chaos has been banished], a vineyard of wine, sing of it! / I, the Lord, am its keeper; / I water it every moment / Lest anyone damage it, / I guard it night and day." Then, "In the days to come

Jacob will take root, / Israel will blossom and sprout; / And they will fill the whole world with fruit" (27:6). Here, God's ecstasy sings over Israel in fulfilled hope, because his vineyard is gloriously restored. God is like the farmer who, after generations of disappointment, has finally healed his land enough to see it produce the abundance and beauty with which it was originally designed to flourish. At last, the vineyard is set in order. Beauty and abundance pour out of it like the shining of the sun. God invites us to the song of celebration! The flourishing vineyard tells the story of God's restored relationship with Israel, and through Israel, a process will take place that will "fill the whole world with fruit." God's joy, then, is that through the restoring of Israel, he finds a route to restore the whole world. The process of healing Israel will somehow extend healing to all of God's creation. God's anguish is relieved as he fulfills the hope of the promise "Behold, I am making all things new" (Rev 21:5).

So, Scripture *does* reveal a pattern of extended loss followed by hope and joy, a pattern that God experiences and *allows to affect him*. God is revealed both as the stricken God and the God who perseveres, who won't give up, who rattles our cages to effect our awakening. Why is God so vulnerable as to reveal his being affected so? Wouldn't he prefer to appear unflappable, like Socrates drinking the hemlock and facing death with equanimity? Why, again, does Scripture reveal an anguished instead of a stoic Jesus in Gethsemane and on the cross? Part of the answer, I think, is that God knows that we need some assurance that it makes sense when life affects *us* so deeply. And when we don't handle the jolts like Mr. Spock, maybe we are in good company. Maybe it's all right that we hurt and struggle when life gashes our dreams and bleeds them dry. If life's disappointments cause God anguish, maybe our anguish is normal? If God hopes and feels pain when hope is deferred, maybe our pain is part of our being made in God's image? Further, maybe the denial of pain is actually denial of our image-bearing nature.

Now that we see this scriptural pattern of extended loss that leads by "heavy-laden" paths into joy (Matt 11:28), we ask, "How might this pattern influence the way we look at stories?" For one thing, the pattern of loss leading to hope is depicted in Scripture as normal, as part of the wiring of this fallen universe; because it is the story *God* is living out. The reason we love good-guys-win movies is that the good guys are *supposed* to win (because God wins). And the good wins, amazingly, not by being stronger but by *giving up* the weapons of pure power. Who wants to be overpowered into goodness?

A second reason we love those good-wins-out stories is that the alternative is horrible. Let's say Hitler, for example, becomes the paradigm of the normal ruler! The horror! If David sits in his cave only to have Saul wipe him out, and that becomes the paradigm story, "we are of all men most to be pitied" (1 Cor 15:19). "We" here refers to anyone who has the delusion of hope if the bad-guys-win story is the normal paradigm.

These first two ways of looking at stories could be summed up thus: in spite of the pain of this world, there is no place for being cynical. Hope is one of our most important vitamins. The strengthening of hope that our thirsts are valid is a key element in how stories are supposed to work.

A third conclusion: since life on a fallen planet automatically creates a conflict within us (we're made for heaven, but we don't live there), we are born into a story where a question is tattooed onto our hearts: How will this inner conflict be resolved? That is, how will we handle being made for a better world, yet living in one that is often painfully disappointing? How will we live with a devastating thirst we cannot quench for ourselves? In other words, we are born into a story of yearnings that cry out only to hear false voices in response. We agonize through the frustration, sputtering through many false starts. We pursue voices that later betray us or bring partial fulfillments, tantalizing us without fulfilling us. We hold puzzle pieces that sear our hands with longing. The power of this burning expresses itself in *how we live our lives*. So, we would be wise to realize that we can't *help* but reveal our stories to one another. The trick is to turn the lights on about how we *code* our stories and make them tricky to discern. There's a subconscious cat-and-mouse quality to how we tell our stories. We both reveal and conceal. Why? Because the prospect of being known fills us with both dread and desire. The *dread* is that we become known, and that the vulnerability of being known will become a weapon against us. The *desire* is that we become known, and that the vulnerability will be honored so that love is the outcome. Love is the goal of every authentic story, which is another way of saying that love quenches our true thirst.

Not only, then, is there hope that our thirsts are valid, but there is also hope that our thirsts will be quenched. Love will quench them, and "God is love" (1 John 4:8).

Fourth, then, new stories will involve an element of risk. The risk is that of vulnerability and hope. Since our old stories are built around minimizing risk, they erode the person God created us to be. Automatically, then, those stories become defensive bunkers, suffocating the new self that God invites us to be and helps us to become. A new self can't grow in an old story any more than a butterfly can grow yet remain a caterpillar. The new self needs the "light and air" of God's new story in order to grow.

Now that we have some foundation for understanding the importance of stories, we need to focus on this idea of the new self to which I just alluded. Exploring the concept of the new self will also lead us to an understanding of why love is the goal of authentic stories, as I said two paragraphs ago. Love is the goal of authentic stories in that our longing for a happy ending demonstrates our thirst for felicity and our dread of dissolution. Briefly, felicity is good fortune, the sense of life's being founded on the hope for blessing. Dissolution is the tendency toward coming apart, falling to pieces, disintegrating with the outcome of falling toward what I'd call a zero state (being a vapor, a nobody, *feeling* like "a zero"). For a story to be true to the nature of things, it must be a story that highlights our longing for felicity, exposes our fear of dissolution, or focuses on the interplay of both. What would love do but seek to understand where another's heart is located on the felicity-dissolution continuum? How could love do otherwise? How could love ignore such vital coordinates? How could love leave another's well-being *that* untended? If these questions aren't at the core of my stance toward another, then I don't love that person.

The journey from the dissolution side of the continuum to the felicity side is costly (which is to say that love is costly). The journey involves a quest for a lifeworld that brings the hope of wholeness

STUCK

(the foundation for felicity). But, "hope deferred makes the heart sick" (Prov 13:12). Our fear of heartsickness shuts us down because, by reason of our fallen-ness, we perceive this heartsickness as "unto death," as Kierkegaard said.[2] Once hope turns into heartache, we foolishly blame hope itself. We persuade ourselves that the journey from dissolution to felicity is a fool's errand. We insist that hope is stupid, senseless, silly. Vulnerability, we maintain, is for the vacuous. The way we express this is by thinking, "I got my hopes up; that was stupid," or "I trusted, and what a fool I was."[3]

But can this be true? Should we really avoid hope? Should we really avoid trust? In answer, a story: Not long ago, I repaired to a coffee shop for some peace, quiet, reflection, time-outness. While I was enjoying these things (and some coffee), a woman and her little girl (about six years old) walked in. The woman went to the counter to order, and the little girl found a bit of space not far from her mother and, without so much as a "How do you do?" began to twirl. She whirled around a point with her arms out to each side. The soul of happy spontaneity. She saw me looking at her, gave a tiny shrug, grinned, and kept twirling, as if to say, "Of course I'm adorable, and I like that you like me." I was delighted that she felt totally safe and kept on twirling. Assuming that there is a young girl twirling in the heart of every woman, and assuming that the vulnerability in that twirling will be used against her more than once (in this fallen world, that *will* be the case), should I have, in an alarmed voice, said to the girl in the coffee shop, "Stop that right now! Stop that twirling! Stop that innocence! It will only get you hurt. I'm telling you for your own good, you little fool. Stop it immediately!"? *Should* I have said that? Would I have been doing her a favor? Should I have made sure she understood that hope is an illusion?

When we find that Scripture says, "Hope deferred makes the heart sick," it intends to draw us to the next line: "But desire fulfilled is a tree of life" (Prov 13:12). When we realize the parallel design of these two lines, we see that hope is still the theme (this time the word is "desire") in the second line. That line suggests that not *all*

---

2. Kierkegaard, *Fear and Trembling*, 146.
3. Paraphrased from Kaufman, *Shame*, 14.

hope is deferred, that our hearts aren't *always* made sick. There is hope for hope, after all. In fact, the word "desire" is the translation of a Hebrew word that suggests longing—that suggests a puzzle piece looking for its match.[4] Desire is an incompleteness looking for fulfillment. The word "fulfilled" in Hebrew means "to enter"—that is, it expresses the idea of something missing that now shows up.[5] Something fulfilling has entered. The idea of "desire fulfilled," then, could be paraphrased something like this: "A hope searching for help waves the joy flag, because its match just arrived!"

Let's look at this verse more deeply, this story of hope deferred along with hope fulfilled. Let's look at it using a thought experiment: Imagine the little girl twirling in the coffee shop. Now she is growing up. Now she goes through puberty, begins developing into a young woman. Her father, absent at work most of the time—even absent when he's present—becomes a place of pain and loss in her heart. Hope deferred. She's seventeen now, a rising senior, when she heads off to the senior-high week at a summer camp. Her longing for affirmation from a man focuses on one of the male counselors, a college student three years older than she. He notices her, too. He finds her attractive; he notices her interest in him, her attentiveness. He knows the line between counselor and camper, but one night the two of them are thrown together alone, and he kisses her. Now she is twirling again. In that kiss she blossoms with desire, hope, longing, a sense of her own beauty and solidness; something is imparted to her that fulfills her hope and answers her question "Does anyone see me? Will anyone love me?"

The next day, the counselor keeps his distance. The rest of the week, he is polite but formal. Her heart begins to collapse: Was it all an illusion? Was he lying to her in his affection? Did he just steal from her and leave her? She goes home confused. She writes him letters at camp. He never answers. The door opened by his responsive, affectionate yes to her is now closed. Hope is deferred. Her heart is sick. Her story is blighted.

---

4. Koehler et al., *Hebrew and Aramaic Lexicon*, 20.

5 Koehler et al., *Hebrew and Aramaic Lexicon*, 113.

STUCK

Now, how would you respond when I wonder whether I should have sternly rebuked the little girl for twirling? Should the coffee shop have become a place she could look back on as saving her a lot of heartache, because there she learned not to get her hopes up in the first place? Was she wrong to hope for her father's love and involvement? Was she wrong, too, to respond to the counselor's giving her a kiss? Granted that his kissing her was deeply wrong, was she, nonetheless, not right to sense something of affirmation in it?

Once she realized there would be no letter from him, was it time for her to shut down her hope in general? To say, "That's the last time I'll ever open my heart"? Should she camp out in "hope deferred makes the heart sick" and give up on vulnerability? Should she stay away from the possibility of "desire fulfilled" like the plague?

CHAPTER 4

Liberation

Maybe we can begin forming some answers based on the three sets of Scripture we've collected: Ps 57, Isa 5 and 27, and Prov 13:12. The stories of the man in the cave (David); of God's pain and joy in journeying with his beloved, Israel (the vineyard); and of hope deferred followed by desire fulfilled—what doors might they open for us?

Each story begins with the tension between desire and fulfillment. David, for example, desires deliverance and safety; God desires a faithful response from his people; hope desires to move from being a question mark to an exclamation point: fulfillment! The tension is significant; it matters deeply whether or not deliverance comes. David doesn't feel at all casual about whether or not God comes through; he is taut with outcry.

Another way to speak of tension is that each story involves waiting. And do we hate to wait! Waiting is a toothache in the soul. Waiting tells us that we are not in control. Waiting contradicts the American and Western ideology of instant competence; i.e., that everyone is a gifted nonesuch who can follow his or her dream without let or hindrance. The positive thinking that dominates contemporary life avers that all we have to do is visualize it to do it. *O, The Oprah Magazine*, for example, reports success stories as avidly as any ministry newsletter spreads the word about its impressive record of converts. But there is a downside to this stance, as Barbara Ehrenreich has seen:

STUCK

> So the seeker who embraces positive theology [positive thinking syncretized with theology] finds him- or herself in a seamless, self-enclosed world, stretching from workplace to mall to corporate-style church. Everywhere, he or she hears the same message—that you *can* have all that stuff in the mall, as well as the beautiful house and car, if only you believe that you can. But always, in a hissed undertone, there is the darker message that if you don't have all that you want, if you feel sick, discouraged, or defeated, you have only yourself to blame. Positive theology ratifies and completes a world without beauty, transcendence, or mercy.[1]

"Visualize it then do it" collapses the gap between ability and inhibition so that those who actually struggle with inhibitions or conditions that defeat them are tyrannized into silence by the media's touting of those who "make it." Besides, if "Visualize it then do it" is really a universal law, who needs God?

Waiting, then, is a salutary reminder of our needs and limits. Waiting is the castor oil that rids us of the waste of pride. Waiting is also an eschatological reality, meaning that it is part of the story God tells by saying, "In that day . . ." or "A day is coming when . . ." David waits in the cave. God waits for Israel's repentance. Hope waits for the arrival of fulfillment.

We could say, then, that the restrictive side of waiting is its power to show us our limits and defeat our pride. There's an expansive side as well: waiting and tension defeat the relentlessness of time. What do I mean? Let's try to get at it by going back to the story of the girl who grows up and goes to camp. If she stops twirling because the counselor fails her, she stops because time isn't bringing her anything (and, she thinks, it never will). She conceives time as ticking onward through fruitless days. She will forever be the refuser-to-twirl, marking time, stuck in self-shielding.

By contrast, waiting actively points forward to something *beyond* time's monotony. Another way to say it: tension is always oriented *toward* something or someone. Tension arises because of something unresolved, implying that it can only *be* resolved in

---

1. Ehrenreich, *Bright-Sided*, 146.

LIBERATION

the future. In God's story, waiting is never a waiting for nothing. No-thing is already here. Waiting presupposes a something, an impending arrival. While secular time is just one thing after another, waiting looks forward to fulfillment. True waiting is eschatological. No one in mere secular time is waiting for anything in the biblical sense of the word. Waiting for your meal to come at a restaurant is not "biblical" waiting; it's just trying not to be bored while looking forward to not much. On the other hand, when true fulfillment comes, it's no longer just one thing after another. Far from it! It's one thing that trumps every other, stops time, brings a rush of joy. It's Frodo and Sam somehow getting the ring melted in the fires of Mount Doom. It's Mr. Darcy overcoming his own mountain of reticence to confess his love for Elizabeth. In spite of the deconstruction, cynicism, and suppression of hope in the West, something in us still thrills at evil defeated and love realized. We have a secret: we want the deconstruction to be deconstructed. We are all, if honest, still waiting. We are still and waiting. We are still, yet atremble. We have, at some cryptic level, kept up our healthy rebellion against a culture that mocks hope and treats it as an indecency.

Why the powerful, culture-wide repression of hope? I think we, in effect, self-defer hope, because the moment of fulfillment hints at eternity. That moment is like a time warp stitching together the tension of waiting with the climax of completion, the excitement of rest. In fulfillment, we vault over all the intervening strain and let ourselves go, falling headfirst into joy. Tension and waiting, then, draw us forward with momentum toward what Charles Taylor calls "higher times."[2] Tension and waiting engender a time surge, a cresting wave in which we sense time speeding toward fulfillment. On the other hand, tension and waiting *stop* time, arrest time. How can both be true?

Tension and waiting announce that time is called forward as we strain toward our hoped-for outcome. Time *without* the tension of waiting is mere stasis. It is the girl-now-a-woman refusing to twirl; the woman not waiting for anything; the woman motionless in hatred of hope. This stasis is time as a set of empty markers—going,

2. Taylor, *Secular Age*, 54–59.

STUCK

going, going, but going nowhere; this is time as paralysis. It is what Walter Benjamin calls "empty, homogeneous time,"[3] time that moves in its regular way, yet the self is stuck. This secular time is a tick-tock monotony, because "this follows this follows this" is without meaning or value. Denis Donoghue says, "[T. S.] Eliot's arrangements [of words] issue from a quarrel between time and value. I assume that value is a way of breaking the chain of time, one thing after another."[4] In other words, putting a value on something pries it out of the relentless flow of time. Value interrupts time, saying no to the relentless march of one thing after another and yes to this one thing that means so much, this one thing that, by its value, is retrieved out of time's tyranny. Time is made to give up its suffocating sameness to allow attending to one thing or person or outcome, an attending that shatters the drone of secular time. As soon as time is compelled to attend to a valued thing, person, or outcome, it stops (not the stopping of paralysis but of attention); for to attend is to stop. One can't attend—not truly—while on the move. Value is the reason we wait and feel tension in the waiting. At this point, we are both within the bubble of stopped time (standing on tiptoe, as it were, to see whether valuing will be rewarded or frustrated) and yet within time as those called forward by fulfillment's approach (time as eschatology instead of just ticktocking). This stopping to attend and yet living again in eschatological, hopeful time is the young woman turning again to her hoping self, awakening that self, daring herself to hope (think of Matt 6:33 on valuing, and thus attending to, the kingdom and its righteousness above all else that people run after).

Hope approaches, yet we still contend with the tyranny of clock time. We struggle against being paralyzed and tangled in the net of the chronic. We live in a split consciousness between the attentive, hoping self and the auto-functioning self mindlessly slaving away to time's dictates. The hopeful self contends with the machine self. Charles Dickens's *Hard Times* portrays this struggle in Louisa Gradgrind, the character trained all her life in machine mode, yet

---

3. Benjamin, *Illuminations*, 262.
4. Donoghue, *Words Alone*, 129.

LIBERATION

who discovers a hope inside that no machine world can answer. Louisa cries out, "Forgive me, pity me, help me! Have compassion on my great need, and let me lay this head of mine upon a loving heart!"[5] The anguished young woman calls for relief for her aching head—filled with machine-world facts and figures of no ultimate meaning—as she longs to find ultimate things (forgiveness, pity, help, compassion) in someone's loving heart. Having grown up in the fictional Coketown, "where the piston of the steam-engine worked monotonously up and down, like the head of an elephant in a state of melancholy madness,"[6] Louisa has found nothing to fill her soul in the fact-laden, ticktock, piston-like drive of nineteenth-century, industrial, utilitarian England. Her life is both crammed and empty all at once. Might the same be said of the on-off, binary, information-drunk world of cyberspace, a world that produces not nuts and bolts and engines but endless opportunities to manage life that pluck at one like insistent beggars? No less than in Dickensian England do we wrestle with an ambivalence: the vulnerability of hope contending with the protection that lies in obeying secular time's march to numbness.

Our old, self-protective stories reflect this split. To the degree that we cling to an old story, we freeze in secular time, doing the same old things, living the same patterns of self-protection. Yet, even in our old story, we peek over the walls of protection and long for something new (even as we fear it).

Here's a story that reflects this split. An eighteen-year-old goes off to college. The university is huge—forty thousand students mingle there every weekday. He looks forward to making new friends. But somehow, they don't materialize. He finds himself not reaching out sufficiently. He feels a strange malaise, a crashing of motivation, a loss of confidence. So many new situations and stimuli are coming at him that he's shocked on some deep, hard-to-define level. He begins to skip classes; he withdraws more from the social scene. Other students stop asking him to parties or football games. They seem uncomfortable with his discomfort, yet their not inviting him

---

5. Dickens, *Hard Times*, 177.
6. Dickens, *Hard Times*, 18.

STUCK

makes him still more uneasy, which increases their ambivalence about him, and so on.

He realizes that in all his life up to this point, he has been living in a cocoon of familiarity. Unprepared for the stripping away of that insulated life, he is stunned at his nakedness in the new situation. At first, he tries to ratchet up his old coping responses (using intellectual discussion and debate both to connect with people and keep them distant from his real concerns), but he soon catches on to the fact that his old story provided that cocoon of support—that is, the lifelong framework of family and friends. That framework colluded with his intellectualizing, allowing his same old coping response to proceed time and time again. Chronicity, without his knowing it, had smothered creativity. Now there's nothing in his new environment, rife with anonymity, that supports the old coping style. He withdraws for some time, at one point taking a hiatus from campus for two solid weeks without his parents knowing. His withdrawing reflects the split mentioned above—the split between the attentive, hoping self and the auto-functioning self that must, like a metronome, keep to time-bound structures. The auto-functioning self is keeping time in the sense of behaving in the consistent, familiar ways, but that self is proving inadequate to the new situation.

The attentive self must now search for a new perspective. Liberation must involve understanding the difference between true waiting and mere stuck-ness. To what must we newly turn our attention? What have we been missing? Is there something in our story that seeks to emerge? Are there pieces of our narrative that have been denied attention? What might be peeking over the protective wall of the old with a story of newness?

CHAPTER 5
Pendulum

At this point, according to the American story, the happy ending comes. It emerges naturally, because newness is what we want, right? After all, we're the pioneer nation, always looking for new frontiers. As soon as we get a whiff of newness, we'll gallop for it, right? Actually, we turn out to be quite ambivalent about newness, because we are sinners (amazing that sin runs deeper than citizenship in a nation); and the hallmark of sin is its intent to contrive safety and control on its own terms. Adapting to a new story means risking that safety, renouncing that control. But who will risk such exposure? Engaging in life vulnerably after years of living behind defenses—who will go there? Sin is the self turned toward itself in constant self-concern. And self-concern means self-protection. And self-protection means running from vulnerability. And that means newness is the enemy. We live as if in a nervous crew on a ship that sails toward the hope of newness, then swings fearfully back toward the harbor of familiarity. We miss God's intelligence report that the harbor is floored with reefs.

Recent story: A wife tells her husband after twenty-one years of marriage that she is finished with accommodating his angry, controlling approach to life and marriage. It's not that she hadn't made previous attempts to reveal her distress, but somehow, this time, the message gets through. Probably, she is able to convey a new note of determination, of being truly fed up. Another source of her newfound power to communicate is her glimpse of a new story.

STUCK

She sees over the walls of her old story (which focuses on being a nice and busy woman who stays out of touch with her heart) to a story of honesty, of speaking the truth in love. He hears her for the first time, but his resistance rears up at the prospect of working through these issues in counseling. It's one thing to hear a new word from his wife and tentatively acknowledge it. It's another thing to cede control to such a radical degree as to bring in a third party. Notice *his struggle with control*. The husband senses his wife's crossing to a new story and inviting him to come along. For the first time, he hears her distress. Since that took twenty-one years, he has developed many defenses against hearing her. With or without a counselor, he'll have to deal with three things he'd rather avoid: disruption of his control, loss of power (which he gains through anger), and loss of built-in distractions (through busyness). These have kept him safe for so long, they feel like his essential self. "That's just the way I am," he says of his anger, control, and busyness. Newness is not on the agenda.

But isn't his statement "That's just the way I am" a confession of despair? There is no surplus of this man beyond the old story into which he has settled. Yet, don't we usually want *not* to settle? We say things like "I didn't want to settle for second best" or "I felt that I was just settling in that relationship, so I broke it off." Why, then, would we want to settle for a "me" that has no surplus, no potential? But "That's just the way I am" *means* "I have no potential." Can that really be true? If someone else said to us, "You have no potential," we'd protest strenuously. Yet, we permit ourselves to dictate to our own soul, "You have no potential." I'm not talking about mere human potential here, as in self-sufficiently remaking myself. Rather, I'm talking about a creational theology of the new self.

The story of Jesus makes it clear that no one has a completed self. If we're all stuck with our current selves, why would Jesus come with the news of newness? Nothing about us can be new unless we accept our incompleteness. And, since we're incomplete, we're lying to ourselves when we say, "That's just the way I am." It would be more honest to say, "That's the way I've *become*." And even more honest: "That's the way I have *learned* to enact my story, and it's the only story I'm willing to embrace. It works for me, and I'm not letting it go!" Of course, it's not easy to accept Jesus' disruptive way concerning our lives. It is too disquieting. The power of "That's just who I am" lies in its service to the old story. It justifies the old story's insistence that it's the only available option. Yet, Jesus lands smack in the middle of the oldness, bringing a hopeful and shattering message: "Behold, I make all things new!" (Rev 21:5).

In announcing newness, Jesus declares his intent to act as Creator. A friend of mine says that Jesus' intent to create reminds her of Gen 1 and God's creating the heavens and the earth. It makes her want to ask, "Lord, will you hover over my formlessness and emptiness and bring good things?" Here is the cry of our souls. Newness assumes creativity; some thing or condition will be made that wasn't there before. After all, Jesus says, "Behold, I am making . . ." He comes as the Maker. The Greek word behind "make" is the word from which we English speakers get "poem." I'll talk more about life as poem-making later. For now, I will just say that a poem is not just cute or impressive versification—it is a resistance to chaos; it is a winning through of order in spite of confusion. Out of this battle, structure comes to words; meaning comes by sweating out hard-fought arrangements of phrasing. Similarly, Jesus works to bring newness through introducing hard-won conditions that were not there previously. "Behold, I am making all things new" comes at the end of one of the most violent books in the Bible, the book of Revelation. Why is it violent? Because it is the story of love fighting for humanity not to go over the cliff of dissolution. The forces for dissolution are furious and implacable. They surrender neither to appeasement nor appeal. So, the book of Revelation (and in some sense, the whole Bible) is the story of a war.

So, when Jesus says, "Behold, I am making all things new," he speaks in the context of a war. It's tantamount to saying, "I have won out over enemies. I have overcome resistance. I have reclaimed what was lost. Because I love, I have fought." The story of Jesus' creativity is also the story of love's victory. Liberation is Jesus' gift to us. In the safety of his love, we are set free from the old, paralyzing, sinful script of self-protection. "It was for freedom that Christ set us free," says Paul (Gal 5:1). Freedom is his gift to beloved children, and it includes the liberation from the old story that we explored in the last section.

STUCK

Why would liberation from sin (about which we often hear) imply liberation from our old story (about which we don't)? The answer lies in *sin's propensity to separate*. Sin divides us from God, others, and ourselves. How? Sin can be thought of as rooted in three forces: pride, anxiety, and sensuality. The strain of keeping these forces in balance requires such a fever of concentration that the effort of loving God and others must be sidelined. This strain constitutes the separating power of sin. Let's look at pride, anxiety, and sensuality more closely. Let's see whether we can understand how powerfully they combine to trap us in our old story.

First, pride—it is that exalted, self-reliant faith in ourselves to make life cough up the outcomes we demand. A story makes the point: Napoleon Bonaparte was conversing with Laplace and asked the famous mathematician, "What about God?" To which Laplace answered, "Sire, I have not needed this hypothesis."[1] Laplace's contemptuous dismissal of God expresses perfectly the arrogance that sees God as superfluous, like a tutu on a rhino. This perspective also relegates believers to rhinos-wearing-tutus status. The feeling toward them is "You can wear a tutu if you want, but you look ridiculous. I divest myself of such inanities and go on to make life submit to me as best I can or die trying." Pride is the heart constantly moving in self-concern and self-monitoring in response to its deepest question: "How close to optimal is my project of making life work the way me, myself, and I think it should? Am I gaining or losing ground?" This is the voice of pride, since it conveys the following assumption: "I have what it takes to bend life to my will. And, since that's true, God is merely a crutch for the weak" (or "I may keep him in my back pocket for a rare emergency"). The result is activism: pride drives one to prove that he or she can make life yield outcomes that validate the self.

Second, anxiety, which is the niggling uncertainty that comes along with pride. Why do pride and anxiety intertwine? Pride commits to wrestling life to the ground while anxiety questions, "Have I bitten off more than I can chew?" Pride is a gambler. It wagers our powers against those of life. It lays a fearsome bet that

---

1. Taylor, *Sources of the Self*, 324.

self-protection will defeat any forces that get in our way. Anxiety, on the other hand, creeps in when we begin to *realize* the sheer strength of the powers ranged against us. Anxiety is the secret voice that says, "Life is bigger than I. Maybe I've outmarched my supply lines. I'm not sure I can cope. I'm not sure I can produce the outcomes in which I'm totally invested. I'm playing poker with life; I'm all in, and I've got nothing in reserve. The next move by my opponent could be disastrous." Anxiety takes the activism generated by pride and laces it with inner uncertainty and agitation.

Third, sensuality, which is the response to anxiety that says, "I need something to soothe me." Anxiety is taxing, draining, debilitating. Sensuality proposes a solution: "Indulge in some form of quick-fix relief, and that anxiety will cool down for a while." Sensuality, then, is our reaction to the worm of uncertainty in the apple of pride, a worm I'm calling anxiety. A worm in an apple? Gross! Sensuality gets rid of it through direct soothing. Sensuality returns pride to its normal self-assurance. The problem with sensuality is twofold: one, it only provides temporary relief; two, the next time around, we'll need ever so much more of a sensual charge to produce the same level of relief. The first means that anxiety will always return. The second means that sensuality itself becomes a source of anxiety. Now anxiety is compounded: the original anxiety of having bitten off more than we can chew is now joined by the anxiety of needing more and more sensuality to offset the waning power of that very sensuality. The problem begins to feed on itself. The solution causes more of what it was originally trying to solve. But this very dilemma tempts us back to pride. This time, pride says, "Okay, yes, there's a problem with growing unrest in my heart. But that just tells me I must seek a solution to *that* predicament just as, originally, I set about seeking solutions to the problem of life. I can still make life work. Now I just have another dimension of life to work on." Of course, this recharging of pride leads us back to anxiety, and so on.

The relationship among pride, anxiety, and sensuality becomes a prison, *an iron triangle of self-assurance, self-defeat, and self-soothing*. Every point on the triangle creates its own temptation to keep going to the next point in a desperate bid for a solution. This

STUCK

self-reinforcing pattern makes our old story hard to jettison. That is, the old story, structurally speaking, *is* that triangle.

Let's take a case in point, a story where a woman came to counseling for anger management. When asked why she thought she had an anger problem, she responded, "Because recently I found a paper clip on the carpet in my den, and I was so frustrated that I turned over the sofa." "Turned over the sofa?" I asked, looking at the furniture in my office. "Yes, flipped it right over with my bare hands." Why was she *that* frustrated? Because she had cleaned that room, and its cleanliness was supposed to be above reproach. She was living in a story that had become so confining that she had no freedom to explore other options than exploding at an out-of-place paper clip. Her story's requirement of perfection was so imperious that adrenaline became part of her reaction to "failure." Her story began to compromise the health of her body. How had she become so imprisoned?

Remember our definition of pride: that exalted, self-reliant faith in oneself to make life cough up the outcomes one demands. This suffering woman just *knew* that if she played her cards right, she'd be able to hammer out the perfectly clean environment that signified so much to her. She didn't turn the sofa over because of the paper clip on the floor, but because of what the offending clip *meant*. For her, it meant failure, a failure that condemned her. The penalty would be severe. Who would impose this penalty? Her mother, who had been a gigantic, critical voice in her life, a voice that scornfully threw her into the outer dark of rejection times without number, a voice that lived in her head as judge, jury, and executioner.

One would think she'd want to be free of her mother's voice at all costs, but she would not break faith with her. Privately but powerfully, she agreed with her, taking up her challenge to be perfect. She never told her mother this outright, she just lived by this agreement. She had faith in her, believing that her mother was right in her critical assessment; and the daughter had the faith in herself to believe that she could rise to the perfection needed. She also had faith enough to believe that, should she reach perfection, her mother would smile on her. What a misplaced faith! In effect, she made a covenant with her mother in which daughter would produce perfect performance, and she would then grant life-giving approval. The subtle but powerful ruling out of God's perspective grows like tangled weeds. Mother and daughter are entwined in a negative-feedback loop of withheld approval and performance anxiety. Again, sin separates. This woman knows God, yet her main relationship with him is to fend him off. Why? Is God such a traumatic presence that she would not allow him to expose the mother-daughter trauma that is ruining her? Yes, that is exactly her fear, for God *does* plan to act as a trauma when a false covenant dominates people he loves.[2]

The trauma that comes from God is his call that we be transformed by the vulnerability of true relationship rather than our being imprisoned in the carrot-and-stick dynamic of lusting for approval as the reward for anxious striving. God calls us to come to him, to enter a far different parent-child story. God invites us into a story where the "greatest in the kingdom of heaven" are any who "are converted and become like children" (Matt 18:3–4). *The trust of a child* in his or her "Father who art in heaven" is true greatness. Why is the childlike trust called "great"? Because it faces the trauma of God, the trauma in which he says, "Be naked to life based on your trust in me. Learn to love well by believing in my love for you. Love is vulnerable. Love will get you hurt; but the hurt, given back to me in trust, will generate new life." As Jurgen Moltmann says, "Anyone who loves dies many deaths."[3] And another writer observes, "To live is to receive wounds."[4] And what are wounds, then, but signs of life? And how much better off we would be if we could take our wounds as a semaphore of life.

God's call to trust is traumatic to the pride of fallen humanity, the pride that says, "I can make life work on my own terms. The way I see it, any credibility I have in this world is to be hacked from the rock face of life by the durable blade of my achievements. My food and drink are status, control, impressiveness." These offerings—status, control, impressiveness—crowd the altars raised by the gods of

---

2 Lovelace, *Dynamics of Spiritual Life*, 89.

3. Moltmann, *Spirit of Life*, 211.

4. O'Brien, *Cry of Stone*, 181.

shame and guilt and fear. By these offerings, they are appeased. To leave these gods' altars empty is also a trauma, but a far different kind from the merciful trauma of God.

Our doggedly constructed stories of self-protection reflect the pressure of living between two traumas: God and idols. We develop these self-protective stories because we believe we can manage the trauma of idolatry better than the trauma of God. Again, our faith is misplaced.

Can we have made a wise choice in opting for self-protection? *The difference between the two traumas is this:* the trauma of keeping the gods' altars supplied is endless and increasing; while the trauma of God diminishes as we realize that he not only calls us to vulnerability but also enacts it. That is, God enters his own traumatic experience in the cross.

God calls us to *a trauma that he has already suffered.* He has preceded us into the shock of love, for "God is love" (1 John 4:8). In coming to the cross, Jesus billboarded God's heart as love come to collide. Love smacks into unlove, evil, darkness, twistedness, hopelessness. Love comes to encounter and is inevitably countered, opposed, resisted. Because of this resistance, love hurts. Love suffers long. Love is put to death. The story of Christ is the story of how love really acts. Again, "God is love." But isn't this equivalent to saying, "God is Trinity"? Otherwise, God would exist as love only *after* creating other beings. But God has always been love; it is God's nature. How did God love before creation? In his existence as the Trinitarian God. Each member of the Trinity maintains self in being yet also yields to the being of the other (which mutual yielding is itself part of divine being, and so three is also one). This yielding takes place in answer to the question "What makes for the good of the other?" And this question about the good of the other is love's nature, which is to say God's nature. Love did not begin at creation. Rather, love engendered creation. And this love had been active from eternity past in the Trinitarian circle dance.

Love is trauma because love asks about the good of the other, seeks to enact it, and collides with and suffers from whatever in the other hates the good. Love is creational. Love is battle. Self-protection, on the other hand, asks, "What will enable me to exploit life to my benefit?" Our sinful nature leads us to create stories that justify our self-interest. We end up hiding one trauma from ourselves (that of keeping our idols' altars filled) even while living in that trauma. On the other hand, we evade the trauma we need: the trauma of God, who calls us to the nakedness of love by traumatizing himself through the cross.

Two things, then, keep our life's pendulum swinging, keep us from settling fully into God: sin and trauma. Sin keeps us vacillating through the effort it requires as we labor to balance pride, anxiety, and sensuality. Trauma keeps us vacillating as we fear the trauma of God and hide from ourselves the trauma of idolatry. We vacillate, oscillate, find ourselves pulled back and forth, living a limbo life of daily maybe/maybe not. Life deteriorates into hesitant increments of humdrum, a numbing sameness of decisive indecision.

The woman who flipped the sofa lives a no-win life. Putting faith in her mother and herself turns into a ritual dance full of compulsion and hopelessness. The finish line keeps moving, and her rage increases accordingly. Life becomes an increasing crisis over a decreasing hope. It becomes harder and harder to fight off a sense of futility.

CHAPTER 6

Humdrum

We avoid the trauma of the cross by choosing the trauma of making life work. This shrinking back from God to reach for the trauma of making life work is the pendulum of the previous section. But why don't we find *that* trauma to be distressing? Why do we seldom *feel* the agony of self-effort? We don't because we win the gold medal in an everyday sport called self-deception. We talk ourselves into believing that making life work on our terms is simply the human thing to do. Charles Taylor uses the term "ordinary human flourishing"[1] for our day-in-and-day-out efforts to shape life into the outcomes we want. Taylor himself thinks that imbuing life with the goal of ordinary flourishing is both a secular value and a great achievement in humankind's history.

I disagree, or at least, I'd nuance the discussion a bit. Taylor traces the rise of ordinary flourishing from a historic split: on one side, there were holy folk like canonized saints, monks, nuns, and priests. On the other side, there were regular folk, who kept to a minimal spirituality and supported the holy folk (who, in turn—according to the theology of the time—supported them through their superabundant spirituality and their prayers). For centuries, real flourishing was considered the province of the holy folk. Gradually, though, the concerns of "ordinary folk" came to be more and more valued. Concerns, then, such as income, marriage, child-rearing,

---

1. Taylor, *Secular Age*, 157.

HUMDRUM

possessions, property, etc. became more and more valid as matters around which to build a life. It became progressively more legitimate to aim at what Francis Schaeffer called "personal peace and affluence."[2] Taylor is right in considering ordinary flourishing an achievement in that focusing on such concerns did raise standards of living across Europe and, later, the United States. But the downside of ordinary flourishing is enormous. It promises fulfillment while having no ability to *fill*. As a result, men and women strive after wind, as Ecclesiastes put it in a wisdom book written centuries ago, a wisdom book that actually examined ordinary flourishing and found it lacking.

Another downside of ordinary flourishing is that it hides trauma in a cocoon of habit and hope. The hope is that striving for the goals of ordinary flourishing will eventually deliver self-validation ("I made it!"). The habitual side of ordinary flourishing consists of policing oneself to build the self-discipline requisite to success. One ends up plodding along to a script of routine practices that are supposed to add up to the flourishing one anticipates. Ten years can go by quite easily in this habit-and-hope cocoon—ten years of illusion, of measuring oneself against others. The uneasy feeling inside is the trauma of a broken promise, a trauma seeking to announce itself but which we repress with stubborn faith that ordinary flourishing will somehow pay off. The broken promise eventuates when success becomes a receding finish line.

Before long, we find ourselves in a humdrum life whose routines make it routine. The steering of life through the same predictable avenues is a route to a flourishing that confuses. One arrives at milestones along the "success" path with a sense of having missed an appointment. What's lacking? Why is the heart sad? The sadness is that of a missed announcement and thus a missed turn. One should have turned miles and miles ago—turned toward the trauma of God and away from the trauma of filling the altars of voracious idols. The sense of a missed appointment is inevitable, because we've kept our uneasiness from relaying its crucial message about the lie at the core of ordinary flourishing. The lie consists

---

2 Schaeffer, *No Little People*, 259.

STUCK

of the illusion that the heart can be satisfied with earthly goods. The lie implies that there's no trauma in ordinary flourishing. But there is more than enough trauma, for we watch our offerings burn endlessly on altars in service to insatiable gods. Hidden in the humdrum quality of ordinary flourishing is the horror of a burning that never ends.

Here is an example of the hidden horror: the terrible infighting between a married couple who have conflicting notions of what ordinary flourishing should look like. The husband wants a stable home from which to continue his party lifestyle. He wants the security of commitment yet the sensations of singleness, and he believes his wife should provide the stability while he tramps about having fun. She, on the other hand, wants a stable home from which to have children and live through them. She wants the sensations of validation (through children) yet the security of a paycheck. As each seeks to secure his or her pathway, they become like military opponents with well-defended perimeters. More and more often, firefights erupt as one trespasses on the idolatry of the other. Each becomes increasingly anxious as one plan for making life work bumps more and more insistently into the other. The battles over territory ("You only pay attention to the kids; they're way more important than me!" vs. "You and your party-animal friends make me sick!") turn vicious, and the marriage is spinning downriver toward rapids and rocks. He still demands to be popular and accepted; she demands to become the mother she never had. Both work like farmhands to fill up the altars of these idols. Each perceives the other as interfering with this arduous task.

Most people around this couple would say they're just living life. You know, humdrum. They're just another couple in a typical journey of marital routines and some understandable conflicts. In reality (remember biography vs. theology), they're having a terrible time handling the trauma of filling the altars of ordinary flourishing with its smiling but cruel gods. The horror, I said, at the heart of everyday life is right here, right behind the smiling faces and easy humor. The horror is rooted in the growing exhaustion of satisfying the demanding gods with their insatiable altars. Everyone is worshiping. Everyone is engaged in the trauma of worship (of acknowledging *something* to be of ultimate value). The only question is this: What does the worshiped outcome *demand*? Everything that is worshiped has its requirements. Otherwise, it would be unworthy of worship (for "worship" comes from "worthy-ship").

The issue of requirements may sound off-putting at first, but requirements can be delightful ("I require that you become more playful; I want you to learn one new game every so often"). God's requirements revolve around the word "holy," which *really* sounds off-putting. But holiness, as the Scriptures use it of God, depicts a separateness that heals. Holiness doesn't effect the same type of separation as does sin (that of isolated anxiety). Instead, holiness offers a separation from destructive chaos. Since everyone is worshiping *something*, the question becomes "Does what I worship separate me from God, others, and myself, or from destructive chaos?" Again, are my altars drawing me down a hellish river toward a waterfall? Or are they drawing me to "green pastures" and "quiet waters," as Ps 23:2 puts it?

Again, since everyone is worshiping, everyone is tied to a god. Everyone is in a relationship with an ultimate value, and that relationship (as has been intimated) is transactional. The things we value aren't static; they issue a summons. They make proposals. They introduce transactions, and we respond. They are dynamic. The Faust legend is a good case in point. Dr. Faustus values youth. Mephistopheles offers him just that, but with the requirement that Faustus give up his soul at some future point. The story highlights the transactional nature of any ultimate value. To obtain it, we have to give up something. The valued outcome summons us to sacrifice other values to obtain it. In other words, every idol has an altar; every idol demands sacrifice.

For example, a man is married to a woman whose first marriage fell apart. In the aftermath of divorce, she lost custody of her two children. She holds tightly to a desire to make up for lost time with her children when her custody arrangement allows it. Her new husband, though, wants her to prove he is number one in her life. He holds tightly to a picture where he always outshines her kids, no matter how complex their situations might be. Over time, the wife has accepted that she won't always be able to achieve the level of mothering she longs to offer. Life is too messy, too complex. But within those limits, she is still passionate about being the mother her kids need. On the other hand—even granted his wife's scaled-down expectations of mothering—the second husband won't accept even the smaller overtures she makes toward her two children. He still feels eclipsed and clenches ever more tightly to his need to shine as the undisputed king. His grip on that need is choking his marriage. He would rather lose his marriage than give up his goal to win the king-of-all award. His idol demands that his wife burn her love for her children to "prove" she loves him.

Every human story, then, is one about relinquishment and acquisition, letting go and retaining. The question is this: Will we keep what a fool keeps or what a wise person keeps? Will we let go of what a fool discards or what a wise person discards? And how will we answer these questions—on what foundation? If there is no story above our self-survival story, we will mix foolishness and wisdom with the stir stick of what makes sense to us. But our sense-making faculty is poorly equipped when it slips ever more often into the narrow groove of our demand for control. So, we end up stirring together a brew of life maxims in a cup we drain over and over to our detriment, to the harm of others, and to God's anguish. He sees us as the broken, ruined vineyard of Isa 5.

To illustrate: A man feels he must prove himself by developing an impressive financial portfolio. It just makes sense to him. Why confine yourself to a salary when there are financial instruments that will work for you while you sleep? Why not take advantage of the investment world so that your private world can be less stressful? These common-sense questions, though, hide a deeper set of questions, partly rooted in his family history. For example, he wants to know why his grandmother and an uncle were able to create a successful investment strategy. Is he just financially stupid, given that his investments have not done well? Why can't he understand the "code" that others seem to have figured out? Why is life divided into those who break the code and those who don't, into the in-group and the outsiders, winners and losers? How can he avoid being among the losers? How prove he's not deficient? These haunting questions disturb his peace. He can't get out of the "courtroom," where he stays in a slowly burning panic that the verdict on him is going to be not so much "guilty" as "incompetent." And therefore, in his mind, "worthless."

What has he acquired in this aspect of his story? Nothing but a burden of proof, nothing but a desperate need to give evidence of being valid as measured by some canons of Western culture, nothing but a journey into anxiety and frustration. Here is a vanity that needs to be thrown into the bonfire (reflecting here the wonderful title of Tom Wolfe's novel *The Bonfire of the Vanities*[3]). Here is a load that needs to be relinquished. The question is this: Will I relinquish what a fool relinquishes? Jesus gives the foundation for wise relinquishing by teaching that "whoever wishes to save his life shall lose it; but whoever loses his life for My sake shall find it" (Matt 16:25). The man who gains his life by outsmarting the market can easily lose his life in the sense of losing peace, wholeness, freedom, relationships. Enormous losses.

Please note: Not everyone who invests in the markets is falsely gaining his or her life at the risk of losing it later. Some can involve themselves in investment strategies without wrapping their identities around the process. My point here is that anything apart from God that confers validation can become an idol; and, as I stated earlier, every idol has an altar. In other words, again, the false gods we serve are transactional, dynamic. They have their requirements, and without our fulfilling them, the "gods" don't deliver the goods we have deemed vital.

The effort to meet the requirements of our idols can be thought of as performance pressure, the energy that drives us as we strive to deliver what our idols require. The goal of performing is that of resting in the fact that we've satisfied the idol. The idol "smells" the soothing aroma of our perfect performance and is satisfied. The idol is, for an all-too-brief while, at rest, not angry, not threatening. The idol is happy. We are happy.

But why is it so hard to stay there? If a paper clip on the carpet can represent an enormous threat and bring overwhelming anxiety, then how can we ever be at peace? It doesn't take much for the idol to

---

3. Wolfe, *Bonfire of the Vanities*.

STUCK

awaken its anger, hunger, and demand. Performance pressure lurks about, a haunting presence that stalks us and sometimes jumps us, leaping out of the night of our insecurity. Anxious striving harasses our steps, because idols are unstable and don't stay satisfied very long. They want more.

CHAPTER 7

Poem

Is there an alternative to anxious striving? I'd like to point toward an alternative through exploring the word *poiēma*, a Greek word that means something made, created, composed.[1] It's the term from which we get our English word "poem." Of course, a poem is the result of skillful making or composition. A poem is a creation, and this idea of creation takes us in a strikingly different direction than that of anxious performing. The Greeks called this act of creation *poiēsis*. This idea came over into the Bible. The New Testament often uses this Greek term to describe God's works and our own good works. We can see the creativity in the word when God says, "Behold, I am making all things new." The word "making" here is from the same family of words as *poiēsis*.[2]

Poiēsis moves in freedom. On the other hand, an enslaved heart drives our anxious striving. Our hearts are conscious of power and the struggle for and against that power. Anxious striving is oriented toward death. Creativity, however, is passionate, free, fascinated, oriented toward life. Anxious striving is pressured by the requirements of idols, so that life revolves around an unlimited competition for limited resources. Creativity is drawn by the requirements of the Creator, where living revolves around searching amid abundance for what serves to bring newness to being.

1. Liddell and Scott, *Greek-English Lexicon*, 1429.
2. Abbott-Smith, *Greek Lexicon*, 369.

STUCK

To understand why *poiēsis* is so hard for us to reach, let's look back for a moment. We have been exploring the theme of idolatry. We have seen that it has considerable power to explain our performance anxieties. We have said that every idol has an altar. We saw that idols demand sacrifices, that they are voracious, and that they will not deliver what we want unless we keep their altars full. That is why we huff and puff through life like a one-armed paper hanger, as the saying goes. The demands of our idols harry us dreadfully. This analysis takes us deep inside our anxieties to give us a greater understanding of them.

There is a deeper understanding yet. Behind idolatry is the idea of the counterfeit god. An idol is a pretense, a false god that assumes the ultimate place and value in our lives without the real authority to do so. But if there are counterfeits of God, who is the counterfeiter? The Bible presents the liar, Satan, as the arch-counterfeiter. This fierce adversary (the meaning of "devil" *is* adversary) steps into the pages of Scripture and, without the slightest hesitation, immediately accuses God of deceiving Adam and Eve. His first recorded words are an insinuating question: "Indeed, has God said, 'You shall not eat from any tree of the garden?'" (Gen 3:1). Satan implies that there is more going on in the heart of God than meets the eye. Maybe Eve should take a second look. When she affirms God's command not to eat from the tree of the knowledge of good and evil (Does her addition of the phrase "or touch it" reveal a hint of suspicion that God has been severe?), Satan contradicts the penalty God had described: "You surely shall not die!" (3:4). Then, he suggests the reason death won't come: "For God knows that in the day you eat from it your eyes will be opened, and you will be like God, knowing good and evil" (3:5). In other words, Satan whispers, "God knows something he hasn't told you, and his withholding it proves his untrustworthy character. Actually, a great good will come to you. You'll be like God, and God doesn't want that." Satan implies that God has only postured his goodness before her while God's heart cheats her of a true blessing. Satan proposes that there is a shadow in God. For the first time, Eve faces evil's main assertion: that one can never trust appearances. Nothing is as it seems. A claim is only a sleight of hand to fool the gullible.

POEM

God has claimed to know what is really the case, but the adversary whispers doubt: "What if God's statements are far from what is really the case, what is really the truth? Don't be a fool. Follow your own counsel." Satan alleges that God can be replaced. With what? One's own powers to make sense of life. One's own self-made light. We are like Prometheus, who stole fire from the gods, a symbol of man and woman in flight from God to their own resources. Humans are tempted constantly to move away from transcendence to self-enclosure and a cleverness for making life work.

Within the dim rooms of our rebellion, our resources look pretty impressive. They present themselves in the forms of ingenuity, cleverness, intellect, collective organization, political shrewdness, philosophical wrestlings with reality, cultural achievements, resourceful problem-solving, great works of earth-moving scope, social engineering, and so on. The purpose of gathering these resources into one list is not to dismiss them wholesale but to present them as attenuated shadows of what they could be were all of them bathed in God's renewing light. "In Thy light we see light," says the psalmist (Ps 36:9). That is, God's light illuminates and clarifies. When we open ourselves and our works to that light, we see more and more clearly.

When, on the other hand, we walk in darkness, our works become false solutions. They make an unsustainable claim to be adequate stand-ins for the living God. Separated from God, our resources become counterfeits, and we become duped by the counterfeiter. We feel the gap between our resources and what they can actually deliver. That gap makes us feel anxious; we seek to close it through pride; in the fruitless effort, we soothe ourselves through sensuality. This iron triangle, as we've discussed, is the essence of sin. We move around the triangle in an increasingly frantic search for a center that might sustain our lives and bring us peace.

Forever chasing an elusive peace, we are kept in a state of repressed emergency. I say "repressed" because we find it too overwhelming to face the internal emergency; it tends to come to light in nightmares and panic attacks. Much of our compulsive lunging through life in confusion and disarray stems from our emotional tank's being drained by the sheer effort of hiding our internal crisis

STUCK

from ourselves. It is the crisis of trying to replace God. Again, we are between two traumas: the trauma of God and that of seeking to replace him. We are the gelded stallions,[3] straining but giving issue only to wind.

Here is life under performance pressure. Here is the labor of anxious striving. It is impossible to create freely and beautifully under such draconian conditions. We are like jugglers trying to keep oh so many balls in the air while the earth lurches constantly under our feet. But creating in the manner of *poiēsis*—the poetic making of a life, a relationship, a work of art, a conversation, a building, an organization, a landscape, and so on—can only take place when one has been freed from the tension of existing between the two traumas. Only when the trauma of idolatry is recognized and repented of can the trauma of God become the "peace of God which surpasses all comprehension" (Phil 4:7). Then the human is on the path toward creational living, toward *poiēsis*.

Below, an untitled poem portrays the contrast between anxious striving and creational "solidity of being."[4] Two views of time jostle within the poem and illustrate the tension between performance pressure and creational peace:

> Time is a fabric creature
> Going for your throat.
> Pestilent pester,
> It rips at your shelter
> While it's running, running,
> Running down, running out,
> Tearing air to bits
> Of gasped oxygen, hoped for,
> Gulped for.
> Tick, tick.
> Chest out, heaving in
> Air freight,
> Tick, tick.
> Can't wait.
> Keeping ahead, so less behind!

3. Lewis, *Abolition of Man*, 37.
4. Payne, *Healing Presence*, 54.

POEM

Time traps you,
Tangles you
In skeins of
Sticky, snarling, snaring webs,
'Croaching on airways.
Life ebbs.
You claw, choke, tear.
Time is a fabric creature
Going for your throat.

Tick, tick, tick.
Engorged, each unlatches,
Another attaches—
Elemental "punctua"
Incremental suctions of
Life, life, life.
Tick, tick, tick.
"Draculant" time thieves,
Clocked robbers.
Time is blood.
Get them off!
Get them off!

Put the clock in a Sabbath bag:
Time in a poke,
Poking along now.
No more kicking its goads:
Chronos like a gun unloaded,
Kairos ascending.
Rest now defending
Your heart from
Time's summons
(Smart phones with their
Strafing come-ons).
Kairos be calling us
From the chronic yoke.
Put the clock in a Sabbath bag:
Time in a poke.[5]

---

5. Author's unpublished poem.

STUCK

What does such a poem have in common with a poem like Allen Ginsberg's "Howl"[6] (if you haven't read it, buckle your seat belt)? At first, one might think that the poem above, with its reference to Sabbath, can't share a worldview with the frenetic and profane and intense "Howl." And, in some ways, that's right. The worldviews do diverge. But they also have something in common: a view of man as wastable. A human life can turn out to be a wasted life. "Howl" laments that waste—it howls about humans turned into trash and deposited into cemeteries where that's that. Both poems are creation-based in the sense that both hail from the land of humans-as-made-for-transcendence. *Embracing transcendence* is one of the three foundations for *poiēsis* I'm discussing in this section.

This acceptance of transcendence is the first foundation for life as poem making. Opening to transcendence (believing the universe is not closed) implies that to be born as a human is to enter into a project, that of receiving and living a life that reflects more than merely following one's own survival mandates. As Paul Ricoeur says, "Consciousness . . . is a task."[7] That is, human life is more than just being full of care and empty of reflection, more than an instinctive thrashing about or a robotic march through the years. The work of life instead requires our awakening into a discerning stance toward the events and feelings of our lives. One works to decode the emotions life kicks up in the heart. It is this effort to decode that makes living into a true work, a *poiēsis*. To cite Ricoeur again, "The text of consciousness is a lacunary [having gaps], truncated text; the assumption of the unconscious is equivalent to a work of interpolation that introduces meaning and connection into the text."[8] That is, we live too often in routine ways of thinking and feeling, in what Abraham Heschel calls "the wilderness of careless living."[9] Ricoeur encourages us to interject meaning from deep inside through reflection on life. That is, we're to reflect, not react. Or if we do react, we need to reflect on *why* the reaction came.

6. Ginsburg, "Howl."
7. Ricoeur, *Freud and Philosophy*, 44.
8. Ricoeur, *Freud and Philosophy*, 119–20.
9. Heschel, *God in Search*, 141.

POEM

Reflection is the commitment to put situations into perspective, to *stand back and be mindful* about the reasons the situation makes the impact it does. Reflection is the mindset of looking for meaning, especially that which isn't immediately apparent. Reflection puts something between me and the situation. Reflection mediates between me and the situation with thought, prayer, worship, Scripture, fellowship. In other words, by reflecting, I bring another thought world into play so that I'm not alone with the situation. I realize that someone else outside me—indeed, transcending the universe—has a perspective about my situation. I sense an overarching transcendence, a strong person who has taken my situation in life into account. In fact, I find that God has *given* an account of my situation, an account that calls my own account of it to give an account of itself. This wording is more than just verbal acrobatics. Rather, the wording breathes out the idea of story, an *account* of events that makes sense of them. I find as I reflect, then, that this thought world of Scripture, prayer, etc., gives a superior and orienting account of my own smaller account of my life. God's overarching story calls my smaller story to the bar, so to speak, so that I find it to be challenged by new meanings. I find that the universe is open, that my story is not closed but rather is summoned to discover that it hasn't the right to premature closure. Called to remain open to God's future, I find that this journey of life has surpluses of meaning not silenced by my own shortsighted, thin interpretation. I find that I am called to wonder.

Reflection opens the universe, because it leads to transcendence, to God and his "larger story."[10] My little story is like a postage stamp on an envelope, inside of which is an uplifting, enlivening, incredible story. For the first three decades of my life, I ran a tiny and frantic route around and around the postage stamp, trying to redesign it, to make it impressive. How foolish I was! Forget the stamp! Open the letter and drink in the words of life from God's wild and loving intrusion onto the darkest planet, Earth. Reflecting on God's mighty and truthful words frees us from the chore of postage-stamp upgrades and upkeep. Our eyes open to wonder—the

---

10. Crabb, "School of Spiritual Direction," 24.

wonder that God asks us a question, which is "Will you let me tell you who you are?" We're invited to a new identity captured well in the words of Ps 116:7: "Return to your rest, O my soul, / For the Lord has dealt bountifully with you." God's bountiful dealing with us through the good news of Jesus Christ opens a restful door. We move from "self-construction"[11] to God's real journey for us: soul making. The journey toward greatness of soul requires God's creative *poiēsis* in our hearts.

A second foundation for *poiēsis* is that *life is not meant to run on anxiety but on affirmation*. A human journey can be driven along by anxiety, but for it to become a human *life*, it must be called into the yes implied by the fact that we are transcended in order to be blessed. Someone arcs over us in order to draw us into a sweeping story with a joyous ending. Because the ending is good, it implies that we are born into a cosmos with yes at its heart. Anxiety, on the other hand, implies a world where, after desperate search, yes is cruelly absent. The result? We are abandoned and desperate. We are anxious.

This second foundation (anxiety vs. affirmation) brings us to the edge of a wasteland, as both the Bible and T. S. Eliot put it. What is this land? As I said earlier, both the poem above and Ginsberg's disturbing "Howl" (not to overlook Eliot's *The Waste Land*[12]) proceed from the assumption that a human life can be wasted, and that humans-as-waste is a grave tragedy. God is not willing for it to happen, but many humans are. Every act that preys on another person by turning that person into something of use is an act of wastage, of disposal, of flushing the other down the sewer. Human history is filled with such waste, but the era of modernity (from roughly 1800 to the present) has seen a massive burgeoning of the waste-one-another mentality. We stand, then, on the edge of a wasteland that, about two hundred years ago, began to spread faster than ever it had in the human story. Why?

The modern era represents a shift to the preeminence of technology. Fascination with technology has led humankind to ask,

---

11. Griffis, "Not a Question," 36.
12. Eliot, *Waste Land*.

POEM

"How can we fix the world with our ingenuity and avoid God in the process?" This question is, at its heart, an anxious one. Its anxiety is based both in its proposal to do without God and its biting off more than it can chew (fixing the world unassisted). Now, a key feature of anxiety is its urge to spread its intensity to others. Anxiety is too intense otherwise. Now the anxious human quest to replace God stands in league with the human "illusion of technique";[13] and we can detect, as a consequence, enormous shifts of anxiety's energies onto others. These are often culture-wide shifts of the burdens of anxiety. They are often lethal. So, we have six million dead Jews as Hitler's anxiety over Aryan identity looked for a scapegoat, not to mention the total of a hundred million dead in World War II. We have twenty million dead Russian peasants, vaporized on account of Stalin's anxiously looking for a way to vindicate the Soviet system. We have the Turkish genocide of one to two million Armenian Christians in the late nineteenth and early twentieth centuries. We have the many who died or were maimed as the English Industrial Revolution—anxious for human grist for its inhuman mills—ground its way over the bodies of the poor and children. We have the dead of Darfur. We have the dead of tens of millions of abortions. I am not attempting to replace history with psychology here. That is, my hypothesis about the role of anxiety in cultural choices does not dismiss the historical forces at work. It simply adds another one—that of anxiety as having a tendency to pervade cultures and to shift its burden to other, weaker entities.

The result? Never have humans been as disposable as in modernity.

Anxiety looks for a scapegoat, for someone on whom to shift its burden (anxiety is a heavy load). When a whole culture asks, "How can we fix ourselves yet free ourselves from God?" the anxiety is palpable, crippling, viral. It is our very atmosphere. Every day, we awaken into a low-lying fog of culture-wide anxiety, a dread that we won't find the solutions. We awaken into a drivenness, a mad push for self-healing, a striving that nags at our longing for peace, a mob of jostling concerns that seethe inside without becoming clear.

---

13. Barrett, *Illusion of Technique*, 29.

STUCK

Just as a fish doesn't know it's wet, we don't know how drenched with dread is the human story at this point in its unfolding. We can hear the dread every day on talk radio, for example, as pundits vie with one another in pronouncing diagnosis and cure. The relentlessness of this conversation is only outstripped by its fruitlessness. For example:

Pundit 1 (speaking fast and self-assuredly): "Some key Republicans obviously voted against their own bill in order to preserve their right to reintroduce the bill later on in a special session when the Democrats are looking the other way."

Pundit 2 (speaking fast and self-assuredly): "But the Democrats clearly understood the tactics of those across the aisle and countered in subcommittee by a floating vote on the basis of the adjuvant committee."

Pundit 1 (same style): "That's scary business, though, when you take into consideration that you can only be an adjuvant when you have a supermajority in the second quarter of a financial downturn. What if the economy takes an uptick and the farm subsidies come up for the renewed spatchcockle[14] option?"

Pundit 2 (not missing a beat): "Well, then, the Democrats either punt or take to the barricades, metaphorically speaking. But this happened before, in 1949, and Truman responded by putting together his famous 'adjuvant-busting' cabinet, a maneuver he based on Adlai Stevenson's dissertation *Adjuvant-Resistant Strategies: Cabinets and End-Runs on Congress*."

Pundit 1: "But you have to understand: Stevenson plagiarized that material, never got his PhD, and falsified his curriculum vitae to get his first job in the Roosevelt administration. He never grasped what adjuvants were about."

Talk-show host (in an isn't-this-fascinating tone): "Next, more on the efforts of some bipartisan members of Congress to blame the oil spill on the proliferation of flesh-eating bacteria in the foundations of homes with lead-based paint."

---

14. "Spatchcock" is a culinary term. I'm lifting and adapting it from there to the realm of politics, using "spatchcockle" as a fun, imaginative word to convey the sense that much of the talk in our culture only pretends to mean something.

POEM

Ridiculous examples, yes. Caricatures, yes. But the tone of anxious proclamation and head-spinning fast-talk creates the illusion that, not too far away, there exists a horizon of solutions. We humans are advancing—no matter how slowly and crabwise—inexorably to claim it. The myth of progress works in the background, bringing a sense that a tantalizing fulfillment is not too far off. An immanent eschatology is imminent, if we can only keep talking. In a perversion of Descartes, our era says, "I talk, therefore I am."

This second foundation for *poiēsis* we've termed "anxiety vs. affirmation." Why affirmation? Because our hearts are made for yes. Here, I mean yes to these questions: "Is my existence a loved existence?" "Is my being on the planet a delight to anyone?" "Is there a habitable atmosphere here, emotionally speaking?" "I've shown up—am I welcomed?" The "wasteland" answers with variations of no. No, it's not good that you are here per se, but if you're useful, you might *rent* a spot. And you might keep that spot if you continue to perform impeccably well. Here, a healthy concern for excellence is turned into anxious striving. I hear this anxious push in the pastor who said, "I guess I'll never be one of those mega-church pastors." What he meant was that since he hadn't been able to generate ever-increasing attendance, he was a failure. His existence was tenuous, doubtful in validity—or so he felt.

Affirmation comes against this anxiety, this doubt. The Creator God is our Father, who says the yes that is sufficient for the longings in the human heart. As Ricoeur says, "Man is the Joy of Yes in the sadness of the finite."[15] That is, humans are the ebbing and flowing conflict between deprivation, loss, and helplessness on one hand (the no) and abundance, retrieval, and love on the other (the yes). The human is the conflict between scarcity and generosity, between despair and hope, between the outer darkness and the feast.

When Jesus has the master in the parable say to the two faithful servants, "Enter into the joy of your master" (Matt 25:21, 23), he depicts an end to the conflict. A new time and set of conditions are coming when full intimacy with the living God will be granted and the "sadness of the finite" will end. Need, regret, and

---

15. Ricoeur, *Fallible Man*, 140.

STUCK

unfulfilled desire will dissolve in the joy of abundance, retrieval, and everlasting love. In the meantime, need, regret, and unfulfilled desire inject urgency into life, an urgency that burns like venom. The antivenin is God's peace, the gift of *shalōm* that comes through salvation. We are saved not just from hell but from "the hell of self and self-consciousness."[16] We are saved by God's yes from the hell of wrestling with a no we cannot master.

The third foundation for *poiēsis* is *God's promise of rest*. Turning life into a poem requires some sense that it is more than an empty and/or harsh cycle. Life needs the hope that one can arc toward home. The ideas of rest and home are, for my purposes, synonymous. The idea of home is such an important theme that Scripture captures it in several metaphors ("green pastures" [Ps 23:2] and "many mansions" [John 14:2], to give two examples). Another metaphor for home that perhaps hasn't received as much attention is that of the "broad place." Job 36:16 says that God wants to place us "into a broad place where there was no more cramping" (ESV). What is this "broad place"? It is a place away from confinement, pinching, narrowness, and enslavement. The broad place is where there is "no more cramping." Conditions there make for freedom, joy, release, unfettered movement, and dance. The large space is safe.

A strong voice about the broad place is that of Jurgen Moltmann. For him, the metaphor of the broad place conveys release from affliction—that narrow, pinching condition of stress, loss, and pain. The broad place is God's providing an open, hopeful renewal of the human, a renewal that calls our hearts home to God so that he is glorified. God reveals his radiant goodness by overcoming the "principalities and powers" that blanket God's creation with the no of hopelessness and nihilism. Moltmann sees the Holy Spirit as crucial in creating the broad place of freedom and hope. In Moltmann's *The Spirit of Life*, he connects the Hebrew word for "spirit" (*rŭach*) with the verb *rewah*. Moltmann cites a study by Helen Schüngel-Straumann that says, "The term [*rŭach*] is probably related to *rewah*=breadth. *Ruach* creates space. It sets it in motion. It

---

16. Payne, *Healing Presence*, 53.

leads out of narrow places into wide vistas, thus conferring life."[17] Moltmann goes on, saying, "To experience the *ruach* is to experience what is divine not only as a person, and not merely as a force, but also as *space*—as the space of freedom in which the living being can unfold. That is the experience of the Spirit: 'Thou hast set my feet in a broad place' (Ps 31.8)."[18] Or, "where the Spirit of the Lord is, there is liberty" (2 Cor 3:17). The place of narrowness (which is the pictorial meaning behind the Greek word for "affliction") is the place where, of course, there is no breadth. And without *breadth*, there can be no *breath*. The Holy Spirit opens up the chest-crushing narrowness of affliction and blows into our lives with fresh wind, with uplift, opening us up to God's good story and the expansive hope of it.

The breath/spirit of God opens our spiritual airways for new life. God blows through the "fabric creature" called time with its stifling drainage of life. In God's newness and hope, we can finally rest. The promise of rest is not real if affliction will have the final say. If the no of the world, flesh, and devil is the final word, then there can be no rest, only anxious striving against despair in existential desperation. No wonder that "our heart is restless until it rests in you," as Augustine says.[19] But no isn't the final word, because "the grass withers, the flower fades, / But the word of our God stands forever" (Isa 40:8). And what is this word? God's word, expressed in Scripture and climactically in Jesus Christ, is yes to his benighted and sighing creation (2 Cor 1:19–20). God's promissory yes is the home of rest.

Nestled within this rest is God's calling us to join him in *poiēsis*. God's rest implies that the normal human condition is that of untrammeled room for creativity. For example, I had a counseling session this morning about which I had prayed considerably hard. The counselee had made it difficult to connect with her; she had many suspicions, especially of men. I had previously had sessions with her where I lost her, where I could not maintain emotional

---

17. Moltmann, *Spirit of Life*, 43.
18. Moltmann, *Spirit of Life*, 43; his emphasis.
19. Augustine, *Confessions*, 3.

contact with her. She had pulled away emotionally, hiding behind a defensive screen. So, I had prayed for this morning's session, that God would help me create an atmosphere in which I could stay with her, that I would not rush past the entrances to her world in my efforts to invite her toward growth. By God's grace, the session became creative. That is, I was able to hear her heart, to stay with what she was saying, even when it was uncomfortable. She relaxed, and the session progressed into *poiēsis*, where we mutually created new ground for her growth.

Having unpacked these three dimensions of *poiēsis*, I want to make it clear that in talking about creativity, I am *not* talking about the postmodern value of self-creation. We are not to make ourselves, for "it is He who has made us, and not we ourselves; / We are His people and the sheep of His pasture" (Ps 100:3). God is the maker, and we are called to enter his poetic heart, that heart of creative freedom to make and give away what we have made. As Dan Allender puts it, "I'm not advocating a return to the sixties' quest for self-identity and self-fulfillment. This is not a search for fulfillment but for a narrative. It is not enough to find a self. Instead it is imperative to search for one's story. It is not I who must be found. Instead it is God who is to be found."[20]

---

20. Allender, *To Be Told*, 13.

CHAPTER 8
Welcome

When we begin to see life as *poiēsis*, something changes within us. Our hearts begin to grasp that our old stories are not *definitive* but *suggestive*. They mark us but don't define us. We are inscribed by them, even scarred by them; but we begin to realize there is another scribe. As we come to know the scribe, the writer, the author of a far grander story, we see the possibility of joining God in creativity, including a re-creation of our own story. Possibility suggests potential, refers to options, opens up newness. The Bible is the trustworthy repository of the grand story—the story about restoring a sad and broken creation, restoring it to joy and wholeness. In Jer 33:6, God puts it this way: "Behold, I will bring to it health and healing, and I will heal them; and I will reveal to them an abundance of peace and truth." The Hebrew wording of this passage is packed with vast fields of meaning. Each Hebrew term bears so much freight that the possible significances shift and play. The whole verse shimmers. It shimmers with welcome, as we'll see.

First item of unpacking this verse: "Behold" acts as a neon sticky note, saying, "Over here! Pay attention! Look up from your cell phone!" Then the verse reveals what should grab our attention: "I will bring to it." "It" here refers to Jerusalem. That's significant, because Jerusalem at the time was under judgment and in despair. Have you ever felt despair to the point that you were convinced you would never feel good again? This is the pit in which Jerusalem suffers.

STUCK

She doesn't suffer alone. God announces ("Behold!") an intervention, a change, a turn. God declares a deep commitment to a new day. The key Hebrew words in this verse are, respectively, "bandage," "heal" (twice), "reveal," "abundance," "wholeness," and "truth" or "faithfulness." On top of all this richness, there is an option to reevaluate the meaning of "abundance," which, as we'll see, opens an enticing door.

The New American Standard version of Jer 33:6 says, "I will bring to it health." The Hebrew term translated "health" means "to lengthen," and it eventually comes to mean "a bandage" (as in, a lengthened fabric for wrapping and protecting a wound).[1] We get a glimpse into the way of the healing: God will bandage the wounds of his people so that new skin can grow. God is telling us, "You have been torn by exile, by everything that alienates you, that makes you feel like an outcast." God announces that every torn place, every gaping wound in the heart will become fresh, strong, and whole. We will be restored at last. God is telling a story in which we will recover fully, in which our strength will return and then some. Hope!

There's more. Not only does God promise to bandage our wounds, but he also makes a commitment to "reveal." Here, God emphasizes his role as a light bringer. "Let there be light" is not only part of the narrative of creation (Gen 1:3), it is also important to the story of redemption. Here in Jer 33:6, God brings to light the promise of abundance. Our story will end in generosity. There will be a gracious plenty.

A woman I know can't throw anything away. She has added a room to her house to hold the overflow. What is she saying? That there's not enough to go around, that the losses in her life have convinced her that life's main theme is scarcity. Her fear of scarcity compels her to accumulate, to have the density of surrounding materials that conveys abundance to her. She wears her hoarded possessions like a heavy coat against the cold of scarcity.

We live in a strange culture when it comes to this theme of scarcity. On the one hand, we're told that we can have anything we want. We are, after all, consumers (so we're defined); and consumers

---

1. Gesenius, *Hebrew and Chaldee Lexicon*, 79.

WELCOME

don't want to hear about limits. Consumers want to hear about options, availability, perquisites, freedom, immediacy. On the other hand, we're bombarded with "how-to" messages (how to get the best deal on a car; how to find the best stocks, mutual funds, bonds; how to make sure you have the sex you want; blah-blah). The subliminal message is that if you don't listen to the experts, you're going to miss out on all this abundance. The intimation is that we can have whatever we want, yet it's also easy to miss it, unless we have inside information or are exceedingly clever. No wonder anxiety is high in Western culture. Many of the riches of life seem to dangle just out of reach. Ours is a culture of both superabundance and fear of deprivation.

But God *doesn't* dangle good things tantalizingly beyond our fingertips. Instead, he promises and *keeps* promises. This is the driving energy behind Jer 33:6, because its context expresses hope in the midst of great doubt. As I said earlier, Jerusalem has experienced intense despair. She has languished in exile for decades, stripped of dignity, abandoned, torn down, a shambles. Every new sun reveals an old misery. Some have even said of her that she is "a waste" (Jer 33:10), meaning she is dried up, desolate. God is saying, "You think 'waste' is the last word about your broken city? I have another word for you. In fact, several words: I will bring healing, hope, abundance, peace, and truth." In a transferred sense, God is saying to each of us, "You think abandonment (or failure, or regret, or hopelessness, or frustration) is the last word on your life? No! I have other words for you. I will make your life a story about joy, peace, healing, wholeness, freedom. Words like these are your true future. I am inviting you to trust me for this future." God welcomes us into a new story.

Then there's that word, "abundance." There are some Aramaic Old Testament manuscripts that warrant translating here as the phrase "time to breathe freely" instead of the word "abundance."[2] What a wonderful direction to contemplate! If we adopt this alternate phrasing, the verse would say, "Behold, I will bandage their wounds and bring healing (as of new skin); and I will emphatically

---

2 Elliger and Rudolph, *Biblia Hebraica Stuttgartensia*, 851.

heal them. And I will reveal to them a new time to breathe freely in peace and in truth." God is saying that the bad time is not the final time. As we learned above, all those who called Jerusalem "a waste" will be called out as wrong. Do you see the hope for you in this promise? Have you ever felt doubted, not believed in, told that you were taking up space, a failure—in other words, a waste? God is saying that at the heart of the universe is a heart that beats out the protest "Not true!" to all those accusations. God's own heart takes up the cudgels against hopelessness, which is to say that he fights against sin, chaos, the flesh, the world, the devil in a sweeping attack on the forces that seek to take down his creation. God pushes them back, creating a space in which we find ourselves welcomed.

CHAPTER 9

Shalōm, part 1

A word from Jer 33:6 that runs through the Bible like wildflowers in a meadow is "peace." It forms a beautiful archipelago, a vast sprinkle of the Hebrew word *shalōm*; and where *isn't* it as it pulls hope out of the crannies of the many substories in the grand narrative of the Old Testament? Peace is not just the end of hostility between parties, although it includes that theme; but it is also the well-being and wholeness that ensues when animosity is resolved. The merest dip into a Hebrew dictionary under the word *shalōm* reveals concepts like "restored," "just," "perfect," "good," "well," "welfare," "safety," and "health."[1] These meanings enrich its basic themes of wholeness and well-being. At times, it can also refer to repayment, the idea being that there are situations where, to bring peace, some kind of repayment must be made.[2] The hint for our own stories is that peace has come from a repayment that has restored a broken relationship. Love had been alienated and is now restored through a repayment.

The idea of repayment, though, could just be one more dreary story about hostile parties where one demanded revenge from the other and got it. On those terms, the story of peace does nothing to rise above the choking news headlines about ever-escalating hostilities caused by revenge and counter-revenge, cost and counter-cost.

---

1. Koehler et al., *Hebrew and Aramaic Lexicon*, 1506–10.
2. Koehler et al., *Hebrew and Aramaic Lexicon*, 1506–10.

STUCK

But the *shalōm* of the Old Testament points forward to the *eirēnē* (peace) of the New Testament. There, we learn that love means the repayment is made *within* the offended party, and the benefits go to the *offending* party. God's heart burns with a commitment to resolve the blockages that hold back the renewal of the fallen, dim creation. God's nature gives a love that would shatter a lesser being. God is the source of being so that, as that source, he can take on death in such a way that a death within the godhead really happens.[3] It isn't that God actually dies in Jesus Christ, for God cannot die, since he *is* being itself. The closest we can get to expressing it is that death touches the godhead in a real way when Christ dies, and it is death that ends up the loser. God in Christ endures the fatal so that death ends up the fatality. Paul describes the fatality death suffers by asking, "O death, where is your victory? O death, where is your sting?" (1 Cor 15:55). He has already implied the answer in the previous verse: "Death is swallowed up in victory" (15:54)—the victory of Christ displayed in his resurrection.

Given that death can die and does die through the death of Christ, how do we respond to our stories when they hurtle toward death, when they're tagged with many deaths (the death of hope, the death of dreams, the death of relationships, the death of loved ones)? How do we respond when loss dogs our days, and our nights simply replay our days? It is all too easy to feed these negatives into our old stories with a grim "See? There it is: that's my life—a dance with futility!" How do we turn from hopelessness when it seems certified by stacked-up losses?

To help us reflect on these questions, we turn again to "the house of memory" by delving into Lam 3:21–24: "This I recall to my mind, / Therefore I have hope. / The Lord's lovingkindnesses indeed never cease, / For His compassions never fail. / They are new every morning; great is Thy faithfulness." These words sear into us, because they appear in the middle of an entire book devoted to expressing the pain of sadness and desolation. Lamentations is a five-chapter poem in which Jeremiah pours out his broken heart

---

3. Moltmann, *Crucified God*, 207.

SHALŌM, PART 1

over the destruction of his people. Pours and pours and pours. Piles up pain in relentless, harrowing metaphors.

For example, Lam 1:4 says, "The roads of Zion are in mourning / Because no one comes to the appointed feasts. / All her gates are desolate." Then, in Lam 1:8–9a: "Jerusalem sinned greatly, / Therefore she has become an unclean thing. / All who honored her despise her / Because they have seen her nakedness; / Even she herself groans and turns away. / Her uncleanness was in her skirts." Lamentations 2:4 says, "[Yahweh] has bent His bow like an enemy, / He has set His right hand like an adversary / And slain all that were pleasant to the eye; / In the tent of the daughter of Zion / He has poured out His wrath like fire." In chapter 3, we read, "He has walled me in so that I cannot go out; / He has made my chain heavy. Even when I cry out and call for help, / He shuts out my prayer. / He has blocked my ways with hewn stone; / He has made my paths crooked" (3:7–9). And then, just before the passage we'll explore, comes this: "He made the arrows of His quiver / To enter into my inward parts. / I have become a laughingstock to all my people, / Their mocking song all the day. / He has filled me with bitterness, / He has made me drunk with wormwood. / And He has broken my teeth with gravel; / He has made me cower in the dust" (3:13–16).

All of a sudden, a mere five verses later, the clouds break, and the prophet says, "This I recall to my mind, / Therefore I have hope" (3:21). What's going on? Why would Jeremiah lead up to this sudden peak of hope after plumbing such a deep ravine of devastation? Maybe there's a method in Lam 3. Maybe Jeremiah's abruptness hints not at a random shift but at a process. What could the process be? Suggestions of a process might come from reflecting back on the journey Jeremiah has made through his poem so far.

First, his journey to this point has employed *multiple images* to express loss and pain. As we just saw, he stacks up word pictures so that smoking towers of pain convey a crushing finality. The images say there is nothing Israel can do to escape the onrushing invasion, captivity, and exile. The hammer blow of Babylon's military might will generate a tsunami, scouring and unstoppable. But there is a larger issue symbolized by foreign invasion, that of the unwanted forces that interrupt *all* of our lives. The thorns and thistles of Gen

STUCK

3:18–19 express this constant hassle of invasive forces. God says to Adam (and, indirectly, to all of us): "Both thorns and thistles [the ground] shall grow for you; / And you shall eat the plants of the field; / By the sweat of your face / You shall eat bread, / Till you return to the ground, / Because from it you were taken; / For you are dust, / And to dust you shall return" (Gen 3:18–19). All of human life is here overshadowed, raided by an insistent frustration that will harry the human from cradle to grave. Frustration is endemic and chronic in this life.

Jeremiah tells us through teeming images that there is nothing we can do to evade or outwit the thorns and thistles. The key idea here is *finality*. Human planning will never neutralize the thorn-thistle resistance built into a fallen world. Only trust in God can comfort inflamed hearts amid the chaos of incessant bludgeoning. Jeremiah's collage of sketches is designed to stop us in our anxious, self-sufficient tracks. Stop us from what? Calling out from before the exile strikes, Jer 2:12–13 thunders in reply: "'Be appalled, O heavens, at this, / And shudder, be very desolate,' declares the Lord. / 'For My people have committed two evils: / They have forsaken Me, / The fountain of living waters, / To hew for themselves cisterns, / Broken cisterns, / That can hold no water.'" Israel, God's cherished child, has turned from his gifts and has trusted that other goods will be more fulfilling than God's own goodness. Israel coldly rejected the Lord's self-giving, favoring instead mudholes of self-aggrandizement.

In Lamentations, Jeremiah's desolate image mongering portrays what the outcome will be whenever humans spread their legs for secondary loves. The invader will always come. The lesser good will turn out to have the right of putting a lien on our hearts whenever we become its paramour. "Stop!" shouts Jeremiah. "Don't turn yourself into a subhuman by submitting to the power of the gods you've made." In other words, don't stumble into a corrupt *poiēsis*.

But what corrupts *poiēsis*? The fear of death. The work of making a life *cannot* go well without an education about the reality of death. Facing death's real presence brings us up against an enemy that is beyond our strength. Denying that this is our real situation simply makes death stronger. We put our fear of death out of sight.

SHALŌM, PART 1

We make a life that weaves blindly through a dance with death. Yet, we don't—in our deep suppression of the fact of death—recognize our partner in the dance. What tempts us to deny death? Doesn't the temptation lie in our "desires that wage war in [our] members" (Jas 4:1)? That is, doesn't desire push, cajole, threaten, goad, wheedle, whine constantly in the background, steering us toward needs that constantly elude us? If death is the end, isn't our intense pursuit of fulfillment doomed at the last? We turn away from such a prospect, away from the leer of death, and so end up dancing with it anyway. We push death's futility out of the front door of denial only to have it reenter through the back door of reality.

What then? Do we deny desire instead of denying death? I don't see either of these denials (push away death or push away desire) as solving anything. Rather, it seems better to enter into a dialogue between the two. If we are going to die, could it be that death is a portal instead of a wall? And if death could be a portal, wouldn't death want to "speak" to our desires with the offer of a new perspective? This possibility is what Ricoeur calls "the re-education of desire." In his critical examination of psychoanalysis, Ricoeur writes, "Thus psychoanalysis would like to be, like Spinoza's *Ethics*, a reeducation of desire. . . . [O]nly when desire is stripped of its omnipotence . . . [and] has accepted its own death can [it] freely dispose of things."[4] That is to say, only desire that has accepted its limits can freely let go and give, can freely love. On the other hand, desire that anxiously seeks to push death aside, that urgently seeks the mastery of life, will live urgently, being driven by the ignorance inherent in this blind seeking of control. Ignoring the looming figure of death turns into fuel for anxious, selfish striving.

The tragedy of ignorant desire is the pitting of hearts one against another. We return to Jas 4:1, quoted above, where James characterizes desires as "pleasures that wage war in your members" and as having thus become "the source of quarrels and conflicts among you." Ignorant desire is arrogant desire, pushing for potency beyond its means by infringing on the freedoms of others. Trampling the other becomes a habit, one that desire won't admit

---

4. Ricoeur, *Conflict of Interpretations*, 194.

owing to its ignorance and urgency. Only one thing matters: death-defying satisfaction! Gratification becomes the supposed sign that death will never come. The bell always tolls for someone else; that's the illusion.

What then? If the mere denial of desire won't work—and it won't, since our repressed desires return in ever-morphing forms like the shifting shapes in a lava lamp—what can reeducate it? James is not long in offering his answer:

> God is opposed to the proud but gives grace to the humble. Submit therefore to God. Resist the devil, and he will flee from you. Draw near to God and He will draw near to you. Cleanse your hands, you sinners; and purify your hearts, you double-minded. Be miserable and mourn and weep; let your laughter be turned into mourning, and your joy to gloom. Humble yourselves in the presence of the Lord, and He will exalt you. (Jas 4:6–10)

James's thought: "Forget about the house of cards you've built by assuming that unleashed desire will make for a fulfilled life." That assumption is pride's blossom and humility's funeral. Reality dictates that we need a life that runs on grace, and grace comes to the humble. Get away from the devil, the original source of pride; and draw near to God. He is ready to draw near to you. "Cleanse your hands," says James—that is, wash away the illusion that resolute desire will work as both engine and rudder of life. "Are you deluded?" James asks, in effect. "Don't be so double-minded, using God talk yet running on the false hope that desire fulfilled will master life for you. Purify your hearts of such nonsense. Mourn over all the harm you've done in your desire-driven warmongering on one another. Humble yourselves, crying out, 'God, I need you; you are my true desire.'" So James.

Jeremiah would agree. Again, in Lamentations, the relentless march of his painful imagery pushes us through futility to *finality*. Instead of our panicking about the immediate futility of life, we're to push on through the pain of *futility* to the acceptance of a *finality* by admitting our inability to sweep away thorns and thistles. We're to repent of the pride that charges down the racecourse of

SHALŌM, PART 1

life with a presumption of mastery. We are, James implies, to be arrested and sobered by our "going eyeball to eyeball with reality, letting our fantasies about ourselves die a quiet death."[5] Our hope in such troubling of ourselves is that we enter the long and freeing discipline of setting our loves in order. Through this healthy asceticism, we learn to renounce desire's arrogance that sweeps others aside. If untutored desire runs our lives, what can result but a creeping autonomy that saps our obligation to love?

What do we do, then? What, when life feels futile, and we've been bitten by the hidden costs of our idolatries, and agony intensifies? Let's say, too, that we've accepted the finality of thorns and thistles, accepted our own powerlessness to make life work on our own terms. What then? In Lamentations, we find that Jeremiah has been following his own wisdom, that which caused him to urge God's people: "Let your tears run down like a river day and night .... Arise, cry aloud in the night ... Pour out your heart like water in the presence of the Lord" (2:18–19). This permission to express our pain to God picks up a theme from Ps 62:8: "Pour out your heart before Him; / God is a refuge for us."

The imagery of pouring conveys, by definition, a complete emptying. If we aim to empty a cup or a bucket, we don't edit the contents. Emptying is emptying: whatever's in there will come out in the pouring. God wants the same with our hearts. The psalmist says, "Empty your heart before God." We shrink back, crying out, "What if there's rage in there? What if there's lust? What if there's a fantasy of revenge? What if there's a secret manipulation of my friend? What if I've been a secret enemy, unbeknownst to the other? What if there are knots of unforgiveness gnarly as clots of blood? What if fear is my daily bread?" The psalmist says to pour all this out before God. The idea is that only in God's holiness can we find a sanctuary for our own failures at navigating life lovingly. On the Day of Atonement, where did the high priest of Israel go with the sins of God's people? To the Most Holy Place, right to the Shekinah, the manifest presence of God. There is in God's holiness a love of righteousness so deep that it determines that sin must come into

---

5. Hitz, *Lost in Thought*, 100.

STUCK

God's presence for our unburdening. The weight of required righteousness must leave us and be shifted to God.

Not that all we have to pour out is sin (although there is plenty of that). We also have the multiplied losses and sorrows of slogging through the reversals and contingencies of a fallen world. The psalmist opens the way for us to sorrow, to groan before God. We sorrow about divorce; we sorrow about abused children; we sorrow about hungry refugees; we sorrow about cancer; we sorrow about racism; we sorrow about the homeless; we sorrow about the disappearance of species; we sorrow about the loss of wilderness; we sorrow about aborted babies; we sorrow about the Holocaust; we sorrow about absent fathers; we sorrow about children crushed in the forces of family conflict; we sorrow about the disappearance of poetry, the trivialization of art. We sorrow. But we must sorrow before God, or our hearts will die.

With the psalmist, Jeremiah leads by his example, leads us to sorrow in God's presence. It is as though he sees God alone as having the depth, the capacity to absorb the sorrow of our devastated hearts. God is like a voluminous sponge, honeycombed with tunnels vast enough to hold the flood of our sorrow. Pour it out. Pour it out. Keep pouring. Keep pouring. Empty yourself that you may be filled.

Next, after finality, is *acceptance*. Here, I mean accepting the defeat of one's personal self-sufficiency, accepting that one is not some superstar of heroic self-assertion. In the journey of life, there is only one hero: God. Without God, we are overwhelmed. Or we seek to hide our being overwhelmed by overwhelming others. In acceptance, we repent of this. We realize that life is too big for a fallen human. We pour out our hearts, we empty our sins and sorrows before God; and then we accept our inability to create a fantasized story of our own impressiveness. In Lam 3:18, for example, Jeremiah says, "My strength has perished, / And so has my hope from the Lord." That is, my own resources are overmatched. I can't manage God with my demands that life work out according to my terms. I will stop resisting. I will stop being a foolish Samson in life, stop imitating the man who thought his strength could conquer any challenge. Here in acceptance is an invitation to rest.

SHALŌM, PART 1

As acceptance becomes stronger, the next phase of Jeremiah's journey is *silence*. He waits in the finality, the outpouring, the acceptance until he senses a space. That is, he senses an internal heart's room where he can now posit the word "this" (as in, "This I recall to my mind"). The word in Hebrew is *zō't*, which expresses an anticipation, a moving forward toward newness.[6] In silence, Jeremiah shifts from encouraging his hearers to cry out and be vocal to God without letup—shifts from this outcry through acceptance to silence. Now we have reached quietness and rest. Now we have spent our cries and are like quiet downspouts emptied after a rain. Now it's time to sit trustfully, meditatively. It is time to let silence before the Lord do its work. Silence ("Cease striving and know that I am God," says Ps 46:10) is the space where anticipation can shake free from despair. Silence is the space where God might come through the door of spent outcry so that hope might make its bid. A new story knocks on the door of "this." Yet, it is also an old story, something one must "recall to mind" (Lam 3:21). The old story, the old memory, returns as new hope (anticipation). Memory visits the ancient story that Yahweh is a God of unceasing loving-kindness, *ḥesed* that never runs dry: "There is a river whose streams make glad the city of God" (Ps 46:4).

The last phase in Jeremiah's journey toward a surprising hope is that of *turning*. Here, he senses the space created by *zō't* ("this"), that space for a new story. He builds a sentence in verse 21 beginning with the insistent "this," a word that invites us to ask, "What is it, Jeremiah? What is the forward momentum you feel? To what are you turning, and might we turn with you?" His answer is that he turns to the act of recalling. The Hebrew word's basic meaning is to turn around and approach an original destination that one had almost missed.[7] Staggered by shame and despair, Jeremiah has now vomited up enough poison to clear a space for returning from loss to hope, from no to yes. In the first chapters of Lamentations, he was too overwhelmed, like a man overcome by fumes—the fumes of despair, brokenness, sin. Now he has cleared his soul enough to thaw

---

6. Koehler et al., *Hebrew and Aramaic Lexicon*, 260, 264.
7. Koehler et al., *Hebrew and Aramaic Lexicon*, 1427–31.

STUCK

out from paralysis. He begins the turn toward hope. His long effort to purge himself can now morph into a desire for God's faithful love.

Turning is that shift from hopelessness to hope. It's the move from "this is the end" to "this is a beginning," from hitting a wall to stumbling on a door, from massive opposition to meaningful opportunity. It is Frodo and Sam defeated at the last by Gollum, yet seeing his very dance of victory become a plunge into the Cracks of Doom. It is the Ring overcome by its own malignancy, its own dark urge toward victory at any cost. It is the cavalry riding over the hill at the last possible second. It is the last-second surge of the good. It is the nick of time. It is the woodcutter barging in and killing the wolf that bears down on Little Red Riding Hood. It is heroism finding its opening. It is courage overcoming the dead end. Of this idea of the turn, Tolkien says:

> The consolation of fairy stories, the joy of the happy ending: or more correctly of the good catastrophe, the sudden joyous "turn" (for there is no true end to any fairy-tale): this joy, which is one of the things which fairy-stories can produce supremely well, is not essentially "escapist," nor "fugitive." In its fairy-tale—or otherworld—setting, it is a sudden and miraculous grace: never to be counted on to recur. It does not deny the possibility of . . . sorrow and failure: the possibility of these is necessary to the joy of deliverance; it denies (in the face of much evidence, if you will) universal final defeat and in so far is *evangelium* [good news], giving a fleeting glimpse of Joy, Joy beyond the walls of the world, poignant as grief.
>
> It is the mark of a good fairy-story . . . that however wild its events, however fantastic or terrible the adventures, it can give to a child or man that hears it, when the "turn" comes, a catch of the breath, a beat and lifting of the heart, near to (or indeed accompanied by) tears, as keen as that given by any form of literary art, and having a peculiar quality. . . .
>
> In such stories when the sudden "turn" comes we get a piercing glimpse of joy, and heart's desire, that for a

SHALŌM, PART 1

moment passes outside the frame, rends indeed the very web of story, and lets a gleam come through.[8]

The Bible constantly shows that God *loves* the turn and toils to bring it about. God loves his creation, and constantly labors to drag it out of peril. The following untitled poem depicts God's passion to bring about the turn:

> Thump and wash. Thump and wash.
> Wash and wash:
> Carnage. Lumpy leavings like sad spoor,
> Humps of wet, wan sand
> Broken down over, broken over down and down
> Drowned in pounds of battering sea,
> Too sad to imagine as anything else
> But deposed backwash of dissolved hope,
> Dumped and damned, a tangled wrangle of no.
>
> Nevertheless, now uprise,
> Away from sighs of waves' fall
> Surprise of higher reach, oh, up
> Near the dune line: new, fine,
> Tall-towered, castellated, carven
> With ever so tall windows, doors,
> Golden gardens behind battlements,
> Crafted, detailed: shining
> Upsurge of parapets, newborn arabesques
> In upswept curves that steeple in flying flags,
> Pennants pealing
> A high message, a most high denial
> Of no's scandal.
> Can you stand back?
> Look? Imagine?[9]

The first stanza pictures the aftermath of waves, in their relentless power, having pounded a sandcastle into an archipelago of shapeless lumps. Hope dissolves to nothing in the wash of meaninglessness. Life's recurring defeats are symbolized by the

---

8. Tolkien, "On Fairy Stories," 175–76.
9. Unpublished poem by author.

STUCK

rhythmic artillery of the ocean's assaulting of a castle once built in hope. The second stanza begins with "nevertheless," an anchor word in Scripture, one that grounds hope in something deeper than can be destroyed by the batterings of discouragement. What is the something deeper? How does this new castle farther from the waves rise in the peace of defiance? In answer, the pinnacles of the castle feature "pennants pealing / A high message, a most high denial / Of no's scandal." The words "most high" suggest a title of God, who is the Most High, especially in the Old Testament, where God persists in reshaping a self-destructing Israel, laboring over her passionately to re-form her beauty, digging her out like fouled clay from the pits of idolatry into which she repeatedly stumbles. Of course, in the middle of the poem is "the turn," the same shift that we've found in Lam 3.

Finally, Jeremiah declares that God's acts of loving-kindness "are new every morning; / Great is Thy faithfulness" (Lam 3:23). "New" in these lines comes from a verb that means "to make new, restore"—that is, to return something to its original condition.[10] In 2 Chr 15:8, we learn that "[Asa] then restored the altar of the Lord." The altar had been spoiled by sacrifices to idols, but Asa sees to it that it is cleansed and returned to the service of the Lord. The altar is true to itself once more; it's considered new.

A search under this Hebrew word for newness uncovers references to a new spirit, a new heart, a new song, new heavens and a new earth, and a new name.[11] The theme of newness opens the curtains behind which suffocating hope had retired. Hope doesn't breathe well in the downward pull of extended loss, which tends to bludgeon promise and stifle the heart. But newness interrupts loss with fresh realizations of God's loving-kindness: "Yahweh will not quit until a newness is wrought."[12] As I say, newness pulls the curtain that has hidden hope and bids it come out to breathe clean air, to recover, to refresh the heart that had waned but is now turning to fresh life, pulling nourishment from God's character.

---

10. Koehler et al., *Hebrew and Aramaic Lexicon*, 294.
11. Koehler et al., *Hebrew and Aramaic Lexicon*, 294.
12. Brueggemann, *Hope within History*, 37.

SHALŌM, PART 1

Toggling back to the poem, we hear an invitation: "Can you stand back?" The poem solicits our involvement. Take time, it suggests, to create some emotional distance from the immediate hell of hopelessness. Can you "look"? In other words, refocus your eyes. In your distress, you've narrowed your vision to the immediate, bad outcome. Have the discipline to open your eyes to what you're missing when you're tangled in the net of defeat. Even the despair of defeat is a sign that *you are made for more*. Why else would it hurt? Can you, the poem asks, "imagine"? There's something beyond the pain, as a friend once said to me. Look beyond it by using the house of memory. Pain tempts us toward wordlessness.[13] Imagination draws us toward pictures that seek to express the voice that pain has smothered. As we describe the pictures, we find words; and words provide a path through the pain, at least for a while. More of this later.

Why does God love the turn? Because it means that the story is moving from tragedy to comedy, from dissolution to felicity. In other words, *shalōm* has come. "Nevertheless" represents the scriptural idea that darkness sets a trap and then falls into it (Ps 9:15). In spite of its cunning, evil outwits itself in the end. Evil puts Jesus on the cross and then can only shriek in despair and bafflement as death blunts its blade on the hard rock of Jesus' sinlessness and love. The shock of death's energy feeding back into itself defeats death and opens the way for Christ's resurrection. The toughness of Jesus' goodness lies in his utter trust in God, the Father. Goodness this pure has no fear, and its utter security gives no purchase to death. Through Christ, *shalōm* has come, destroying all the handholds of death. Thus, when despair comes calling, Jesus is the servant who goes to the door, refuses its card, and throws it off the property.

---

13. Scarry, *Body in Pain*, 4.

CHAPTER 10
Shalōm, part 2

Has despair left its calling card in your foyer? If you are anything like me, there are days when a daunting pile of discouraging cards loiters smugly on the entry table, the outliers spread out on the floor like kudzu. Here's another iteration of the "tangled wrangle of no." How does such a jungle of discouragement pile up? Let's take this word picture of calling cards farther. In nineteenth-century Europe, one signaled one's "good breeding" by the use of a calling card. A caller would knock at someone's door, hoping to form a relationship. A servant would open the door and receive the visitor's calling card, whereupon the visitor would leave, not usually expecting an immediate reception by the master or mistress of the home. If said master or mistress were at home, the servant would convey the card to him or her. If not, the servant would leave the card in a tray on the entry table. If the master/mistress wanted a visit, he/she would return, by servant, a card to the hopeful visitor.

In our imagined word picture, a whole army of despair's minions have trooped in, leaving card after card with the hard-pressed servant, who piles them, willy-nilly, on the entry table. Now the master of the house comes, clutching his hair, to undertake the dreadful obligation of replying to the cards. The servant having delivered the appropriate cards, the master receives the first visitor. "Your returned visiting card was drab," intones the guest. "This tea is cold, and your jam has a poor set. Too runny. You haven't done much with the house, have you? It's much too dark in here. The

SHALŌM, PART 2

club to which you belong is rather tawdry. They say in the city that it's to close soon." So goes the mordant droning. And that's just the first visitor!

The book of Lamentations presents a picture in which Jeremiah's "foyer" (which is probably on fire) has received an avalanche of despair's cards. He "reads" all of them, as we've seen, piling up image after image of disaster. Then he arrives at the turn to hope and makes much of the "loving-kindnesses" of the Lord. "Loving-kindness" is a covenant word. The writer remembers—after reading a daunting cacophony of dark calling cards—*that God has made a covenant with his people*. The covenant is unbreakable, so much so that the sufferer recognizes it as the answer to his despair. Again, "Yahweh will not quit until a newness is wrought."[1] Even the destruction of Jerusalem must be regarded as a lesser event than God's resolute faithfulness to the covenant he made in love with his people. What is a covenant? An unconditional agreement to stay in relationship. Cities may fall, one's health may break, depression may leap on one like a pit bull, sin may break through like a panther and ravage one's life and the lives of others. Yet all these and more must obey God's will and leave our saving and sanctifying relationship with God unmolested. They cannot touch that relationship any more than the Wicked Witch of the East could touch Dorothy's ruby slippers.

All of these "visitors" will certainly deliver their dark calling cards. But God's covenant means that a different servant answers the door, the suffering servant: "We ourselves esteemed Him stricken, / Smitten of God and afflicted" (Isa 53:4). Stricken, smitten, and afflicted. "We" saw that the servant had been crushed and even that God had sent the dreadful, dark cards that turned into paving stones and drove him into the dirt. But this was *not* the character of his suffering; rather, "He was pierced through for *our* transgressions, / He was crushed for *our* iniquities; / The chastening for *our* well-being fell upon Him, / And by His scourging we are healed" (Isa 53:5, emphases added). Four times in this verse, the servant suffers for our wrongs. Either these are merely pious words worth a

---

1. Brueggemann, *Hope within History*, 37.

STUCK

mere pixel within trillions of pixels—the vast scree of noisy, intrusive information—or they're the before-and-after words that turn clock time into pregnant time.

If they're true, then beneath the livery of the suffering servant are the robes of the "Prince of Peace," or, in Hebrew, *śar-shalōm* (Isa 9:5, which is 9:6 in our English versions).[2] And there is our word *shalōm*. Jesus, the suffering servant of Israel, is the one in charge of *shalōm*; or, as one rendering puts it, the one "to whom peace is entrusted."[3] When despair leaves its calling cards, peace is shattered. But when the suffering servant answers the door with the authority of *undeserved suffering for others*, he simply refuses the card. It has no standing. He summarily closes the door on the presenter. The foyer stays free of the dark refuse.

Then we imagine a holy thing: his princely robes shine from beneath his servant's garb. The table, of a sudden, stretches and widens, loaded with a banquet. The foyer transforms into a great feasting hall. Without formality, guests arrive—the lame, the poor, the blind, lepers, prostitutes, the taxman, the weak, you, me. We realize who actually is the master of the house and take our place at table with the rest of the lowly. Glad of our new title, we gaze at the abundance beckoning all along the banquet board. Suddenly, he has become the servant again and is at our elbow, asking us about the wine. And is the fare to our liking? Generosity, concern, joy.

I ran this metaphor about the calling cards by my wife, and she was honest in her reply: "I'm far from being able to apply it helpfully to my life. It just seems so high a thing to reach." Her honesty provoked me to think to myself: "How much do I understand about this rich idea? How able am I *really* to ward off despair when my spirit is oppressed and gloom settles its heavy, steaming blanket over my heart?" I had to admit, too often the answer is "not very." What gets in the way? As I pray over this question, here's what comes: I can *see* my shattered dreams. They're scattered like bison that ran off a cliff to perish far below. Their obvious remains litter the valley. The beautiful animals will never return. For example, my

---

2. Koehler et al., *Hebrew and Aramaic Lexicon*, 1352.
3. Koehler et al., *Hebrew and Aramaic Lexicon*, 1352.

SHALŌM, PART 2

parents' divorce is long past. My father remarried twice. Both he and my mother have passed away. An un-divorce is impossible now. I can *see* that. My dream of growing up in an intact family? Long gone. And, as it turns out, the dream of my own children having two loving grandparents is also irretrievably gone. It's marooned on an island called Never-to-Be. And, like Atlantis, even the island sank. I can *see* all this. All of us could chime in here with stories of loss that we can see clearly.

On the other hand, I cannot literally *see* Jesus, let alone see him going to the door to send despair packing and throwing its calling cards into the street. Of course, that's the problem with a metaphor, which functions as an imagined reality thrown beside a known reality to bring out the latter's unfathomed depths. By definition, an imagined reality is *unseen*. But its power comes from its ability to act as an accompanying "story" that throws light on unknown discoveries within the known reality. Here, the known reality is the service Christ has rendered as the Savior. The imagined reality is that of Jesus as both suffering servant and Prince of Peace, and his operating in this imagined story as the *different and authoritative* servant answering the "door" in a way that protects the "house" (our redeemed selves). From this metaphor, we begin to *see* that Jesus saves us from more than just the hell of separation from God forever. We see that we live in a world where many powers other than God press in on us with their claims. Like officers of an invading army (another metaphor!), they requisition our time, our attention, our love, our money, our priorities, our values, our dreams. What a world this is! A world teeming with pretended authorities and lords loudly urging their rights on us. Pressing in, seeking to hijack our minds and hearts. We find ourselves in need of a Savior here, too. It isn't just the afterlife that desperately requires a saving intervention, it is also true of this life; for in it are dozens of false lords that bedevil our lives from within and without.

We've been looking at a single false lord, despair, that inundates us with its calling cards. But there are many other such harassments. Our world is a storm of false gods banging on our doors, seeping in at our windows, coming up through the pipes. These false gods can be our own distorted thoughts, worldly ideologies,

STUCK

demonic temptations and accusations. These cries and whispers whipsaw us, harrying us like raptors until, tired out, we settle into some false bastion of rest (an addiction, a power orientation, a fog of despair, materialism, manipulating others, and so on). We live under the sway of idols. Ernst Käsemann writes:

> [Our] final redemption is guaranteed in the earthly present, where God's Holy Spirit is given as the earnest of the consummation (2 Cor. 1:22; 5:5), consequently, by incorporation into the Body of Christ of the church. Even in this state, Christians in their corporeality continue to [exist in] earthly existence under attack. They must therefore tame their bodies, according to 1 Corinthians 9:27, actually punish them; according to Romans 6:16ff., allow them to be made slaves of the divine righteousness. The Christian lives in obedience to the first commandment and is thus continually tempted to want to live from idols, to live from the power and reasoning of this world . . . [T]hey are not yet withdrawn from the pull of earth to emancipate themselves, [and] are set in the world-wide struggle between God and Satan, called to sanctification.[4]

Within this "world-wide struggle," many principalities and powers, thrones and dominions, come calling. They harass us by making claims, and their claims are what I'm trying to shed light on in this metaphor of despair (or some other false lord) arriving with its calling card.

Let's go farther. Despair comes with its claim. Let's say it takes the following form:

> Compared to other people your age, you have fallen far behind. I claim that you are a failure and that your right to think of yourself as good, valid, or respectable is now void. For this reason, I further claim that your opinion of yourself should be full of accusation and disdain. You should also feel a sense of futility, because what is the point of your life anyway? Now you're too far behind to make up for your failures.

---

4. Käsemann, *On Being a Disciple*, 42–43.

SHALŌM, PART 2

Or, "Look at that mistake you just made! You've made that same mistake, oh, how many times? Hundreds? Maybe *you* are the mistake." You get the idea. We're exhausted from trying to answer these claims as they press on us for years and decades. Ultimately, answering them (or quieting them) is beyond us. We need to be saved from these iron laws that clamor, that create so much noise in our heads and hearts.

But we can't save ourselves. Yet, we try. Just as there are false lords, there are false answers to them—i.e., false servants we "send to the door." We might, for example, send the servant of pressured performance. Instead of simply refusing the card, this servant argues vociferously with despair, presenting our achievements, citing our strong points. Despair, challenged, launches a new set of evidence that we don't belong on the planet, and so it goes. A raging and depleting battle at the door ensues, and there's so much noise in our heads we can't hear the true Lord, who is the only one who can deal with the false lord's badgering.

Or, we might send a proud servant to the door to present our superiority. "Pooh!" says the servant to despair. "My master is away at the denominational meeting, serves on the judiciary affairs committee—very busy. Away with you!" Despair backs away from the door, looking past the servant as pride comes in at the window, bringing self-satisfaction and complacency in train. Here, we think of Jesus' caution about throwing out one demon and tidying up. But with no change in the atmosphere of the house, seven demons come back to pleasant environs. As we turn to deal with *them*, despair sidles back to the door and begins a maddening knock. We are lost in a "bog of introspection."[5]

Or, we might send the servant of passive surrender, who says gloomily, "Yes, do come in. The master awaits you in his dark study. He knows you're right: there's nothing impressive here or even worthwhile. I'll send round for your luggage; you might as well stay." This absorbing of despair harbors the odd hope that such sad and sharp suffering might serve as a merit badge to present to God. Sometimes pride and despair work as allies.

---

5. Payne, *Real Presence*, 123.

STUCK

Again, these servants are as false as the false lords they seek to answer, neutralize, or accommodate. Every such servant simply gets embroiled with the false lord in a hopeless dance and ends up under the iron law created by its claims. Even to oppose that claim or try to neutralize it in any way chains one to the law, to the binding pressure to win out over the claim one way or the other.

When Christ goes to the door, the atmosphere changes completely. By "sending" Christ to the door, we acknowledge that we ourselves have no power to resist the claims there. They are at least partly right about us, for "all have sinned and fall short of the glory of God" (Rom 3:23). We have fallen. We have come short. The "glory of God" recedes, and any effort we make to chase it down dooms us to stumble and fall again and again. Exhausted, we entrust the duties of the door to Christ, the one "to whom peace is entrusted."[6] After he deals with the unpleasantness at the door, Jesus turns to us, saying, "Come to Me, all who are weary and heavy-laden, and I will give you rest. Take My yoke upon you, and learn from Me, for I am gentle and humble in heart; and you shall find rest for your souls. For My yoke is easy, and My load is light" (Matt 11:28–30). This is the beginning of the feast!

But I was not at the feast a couple of weeks ago when I tried for two days to fix the ceiling fan in our den. First of all, the fan's model number was brilliantly placed so that it was snugged up against the ceiling, a fiendishly elusive spot. Of course, I had no paperwork that would help. Took two hours to find the model number. It took three days for the company to respond to me with an email regretting to inform me that the model number was that of an obsolete fan for which they no longer carried parts. They did offer me a coupon for a new fan. Nice. Meantime, I had watched several online videos about fan repair and figured out the part I needed. Three or four trips to the hardware store yielded the part. Then it was taking the faceplate off the piece (The what? Cupola? Hangy-down, cuppy thing?) that held the switch and all the wiring. Once I removed it, I was faced with spaghetti. And on it went. After the best part of a

---

6. Koehler et al., *Hebrew and Aramaic Lexicon*, 1352.

SHALŌM, PART 2

day struggling with the wiring, I hooked up the spaghetti properly (I think), threw the circuit breaker back on, and—voila!—nothing!

I was crestfallen. More than that, many loud claimants had crowded to my "door." One of them said, "You've wasted two whole days, you idiot. You should've called an electrician long before now!" Another said, "Most men could do this in their sleep. Look how inept you are! Imagine this debacle being on Facebook for everyone to see. You'd be a laughingstock!" Yet another one said, "Now you've wasted your vacation [I had taken some time off]. What a bad choice! Now you're tired and discouraged! Who does that when rest is so important right now?! You will never learn." Yet another: "You might as well face it. Life just has your number. It can see what you're up to and just blocks you with the merest effort. You're in over your head, buddy." Frantically, I sent both argumentative and accommodating servants to the door. That just got me in deeper. As I tried to resist, adjudicate, accommodate, neutralize their claims, I simply got lost in a marathon committee meeting in my head. The agenda of the meeting was to drive home the accusation "This guy doesn't belong on the planet! Who let him in here?" That may sound dramatic, but in the context of Jesus' characterizing the devil as "a murderer from the beginning" (John 8:44), we begin to understand the intensity of our battle. When we add "He is a liar and the father of lies" (same verse), we see that the voices at the door are tactically placed. The pain of the battle shows why addictions sometimes seem like such a good option: they bring temporary numbness to the electrified thornbush inside our heads.

It was high time for me to step aside and yield the door to Christ. I think of two crucial ways to "send" Christ there. The first is to realize that the full armor of God in Eph 6 *is* Jesus Christ. All of the components of the armor gather to speak of his work for us on the cross and in the resurrection. When we "put on the full armor of God" (Eph 6:11), we put on the Lord Jesus Christ himself. The pieces of armor described in Eph 6:14–18 are but discrete aspects of Jesus. What is the basis for this thought? In Rom 13:12b, Paul says, "Let us cast off the works of darkness and put on the armor of light." Two verses later, he writes, "But put on the Lord Jesus Christ, and make no provision for the flesh, to gratify its desires" (13:14).

STUCK

The armor of light in 13:12b is equivalent to the Lord Jesus Christ in 13:14. In Eph 6:14–18, Paul simply spells out and illuminates the rich aspects of Christ's protective provisions for his children.

All of the dark, clamoring minions that arrive at our door reside on the family tree of the devil. They need not be his direct emissaries to be kindred to him in a distant but real way. This means that psychology is theology. Apart from organic causes, our mental conflicts are the result of living in a world where a spiritual predator still has enough leeway to bedevil us. And what does a predator do but seek prey? "Your adversary, the devil, prowls about like a roaring lion, seeking someone to devour" (1 Pet 5:8). Yet, we are not left there: "But resist him, firm in your faith" (5:9). Firm in your faith, of course, in Christ, which is tantamount to saying, "But put on the Lord Jesus Christ, and make no provision for the flesh"—nor for the work of Satan; nor for the blandishments of the world. Without this firmness, without this resistance, our minds, wills, emotions, and our very bodies come under tremendous pressure. The calling cards pile up, casting us into terrible internal conflicts (like the one I described above, where I failed to fix the ceiling fan). Firmly putting on Jesus Christ in prayer, which is putting on the full of armor of God, is the first way to send Christ to the door.

The second way involves the use of holy imagination.[7] When we see Christ answering the door for us, we're using our imaginations in a holy manner. As believers, we intuit God's real presence in our lives. The Spirit-led intuition (Rom 8:16) helps us to assemble the elements in our imaginative foray into spiritual warfare. There is the enemy: lies, manipulations, and plausible conceits of the world, flesh, and devil. There is the door: they seek to enter our minds and hearts. There is the beleaguered servant: our old responses to these pressures—that is, a harried, grudging admission that we owe them some kind of permission to make their case. This old way is actually an unholy use of imagination. We imagine that we have to fight these twisted messages on their own terms and with our own resources. We imagine ourselves to be alone in a running skirmish at the door. We fail to intuit the real presence of Jesus Christ in our

---

7. Payne, *Real Presence*, 123.

SHALŌM, PART 2

lives, the one who comes that we "might have life, and might have it abundantly" in spite of the fact that "the thief comes only to steal, and kill, and destroy" (John 10:10).

John 8:31–32 tells us, "Jesus therefore was saying to those Jews who had believed Him, 'If you abide in My word, then you are truly disciples of Mine; and you shall know the truth, and the truth shall make you free.'" "Abide" means to settle down and be at home in something, to have a dwelling in a place or a set of habits. When we abide in the words of Jesus that cut through old realities like a razor through tissue paper, the unseen, real presence of God enters our lives and hearts. Jesus' presence brings ultimate and enduring truth, a truth that liberates us. It frees us by exerting a lightening of the heart, the opposite of the miserable, harassing pressure at the door.

Why does his truth have the power to set us free? The answer is complex, but one aspect of it is that for the last four hundred years or so, the growing influence of the Enlightenment's humanity-centered view of reality has pounded into us the idea that our key problem is existential. That is, what are we doing here? Can we know what our existence is for? Is it for anything? Or are our lives simply a meaningless interval between "on" and "off"? How do we solve the problem of existence, trapped as we are in the confines of a closed universe? Do we simply stand in this meaningless interval known as "life on earth" and comment mockingly on those who cling to the idea that meaning exists? Do we just make our own meaning in midair? If the universe is sealed off from authentic meaning, is there any alternative to this existential struggle?

Simply put, Jesus opens the universe: "He who has seen Me has seen the Father," he says (John 14:9). Jesus reveals God, our heavenly Father.[8] Jesus is revelation, and when we see the word "revelation," we ought to imagine "cutting torch" or "lightning bolt." As the lightning turns the night inside out with brilliance, so revelation opens our narrow, one-dimensional world into primordial, eternal light (known biblically as "glory"). Since our earthly eyes cannot see these things, God has provided a way to open the "eyes

---

8. "Father" here does not mean "male patriarch"; it means the one who creates, protects, and gives wise oversight. It is not a gender-designating term in this context.

of [our] heart" (Eph 1:18)—that is, to perceive the Real. And that way is Jesus Christ.

The truth that God is incarnate in Jesus Christ means that our problem is not existential. We *know*—or are invited to know—through the intruding Christ that our existence is a good creation from God. Our problem, then, is *theological* in that it pivots around the question of whether a prior intrusion—that of sin—can ultimately ruin what God has made. If sin has the power of ultimate ruin, then the universe *is* closed, and God is distant. So determined is God that sin *not* have the last word that "He made Him who knew no sin to *be* sin that we might become the righteousness of God in Him" (2 Cor 5:21, emphasis added). Such powerful words! God determined to send Jesus as "the likeness of sinful flesh" (Rom 8:3), setting up a grand exchange where God grants us (the real sin bearers) "the righteousness of God in Him [Christ]" (2 Cor 5:21). Through this gift that puts a lifting lever beneath all despondency, God becomes the one who "justifies the ungodly" (Rom 4:5):

> [God] unmasks us as sinners and only in dying for us can be our Lord, [and] the result is that God's righteousness is justice for the unjust. We no longer have any privilege or claim, thus no righteousness of our own. Only hypocrites or the blind do not see it. Our own justice could only be judgment on us.[9]

The last sentence underlines the fact that "all our righteous deeds are like a filthy garment" (Isa 64:6), and this is *good* news in that it kicks the last props of self-sufficiency out from under us and shows us our utter need. Only in this way can *paupers* be adopted into the house of the King.

Instead of sin running off with creation, God has taken the ruin into God's own self and has defeated it. Our existence, in itself *good*, is harassed and darkened by sin. All our efforts to save it amount to hauling ourselves out of quicksand by pulling at our own feet. This is because our existence is not questionable; it is indisputably good. It is God's good creation; there's nothing more to say! Sin's attack is not on our existence itself but on what makes it flourish: our bond

---

9. Käsemann, *On Being a Disciple*, 42–43.

SHALŌM, PART 2

with God. Separate from our Lord, we wander and become lost. "All of us like sheep have gone astray" (Isa 53:6). Satan seeks to wrap us in a stifling chaos of darkness, but God wrenches the prison open. Light, love, and liberation pour in through the slicing incarnation of Christ as we dance out into "a large space where there is no more cramping" (Job 36:16 ESV).

Notice how much I've been quoting from Scripture in this section on "holy imagination." And notice how our real problem is a problem of theology, of *theo-* (God) *logy* (word). Our problem is not existential but theological. Our desperate need is for words from God. If God has not spoken, our lot is hopeless. Shut inside a closed universe—vast and cold and meaningless—we make up tenuous, self-help stories. These are the matches we strike desperately in the freezing night. Nevertheless, that is not our lot. The universe is as open as a roofless house, because God has stirred up prophets and apostles who, carried along by the Holy Spirit, have heralded the good news of Jesus Christ.

One of those apostles, John, strategically chose to call Jesus "the Word" (John 1:1), thus highlighting our need for divine speech. Our souls are like tuning forks kept still and quiet but ready to answer to the right frequency. God's speech sounds the music to which our hearts are meant to sing. Again: "Come to Me," says Jesus, "all who are weary and heavy-laden, and I will give you rest" (Matt 11:28). In the bone-tiredness of rattling around in a prison-house cosmos, our hearts wonder, "Is there any rest?" If there is true rest, our hearts long to sing along with it.

There are nights when I'm lying in bed, and some car cruises the neighborhood pounding music through subwoofers the size of refrigerators. My teeth vibrate in my head from a block away. Somebody has blanketed the night with some serious sound. I think, "This is God's method. Jesus thunders the speech of God through the neighborhoods, towns, and cities of the world, waking us from our sleep." The piercing, sounding, reaching Word of God is the ground for holy imagination, for now we have a basis for intuiting the Real beyond the real.

Yet, this may seem hard to relate to in the West of the world when a significant swath of people under forty don't identify

STUCK

religion as an important part of their lives. How can we speak of a piercing, sounding, reaching Word of God in a world where meaning is decided not only from within the closed universe but within each person's set of private reference points? In other words, meaning only occurs in an enclosure (the autonomous self) within an enclosure (the shuttered universe). Meaning devolves into something so idiosyncratic that life becomes like a lava lamp: new and endlessly varying shapes of supposed meaning rise, morph, and fall day after day. Within secularity (defined as the massive rise of the "buffered self" in a "disenchanted universe"[10]), the rescinding of God occurs with a roar that drowns out the silence in which God's voice finds a hearing (again: "Cease striving and know that I am God" [Ps 46:10]).

A few years back, I heard a radio report on National Public Radio on an individual who had moved from New York City to Washington, DC. To his surprise, he noticed the screech of sirens more often in DC than in New York. After some investigating, he found that in New York, the combination of canyon-like conditions created by skyscrapers and the high level of traffic noise simply drowned out the screams of emergency vehicles if they were more than a couple blocks away. In DC, with the much-lower skyline and lighter traffic, sirens could be heard from much farther away. New York City actually far outstripped Washington in frequency of sirens. One simply couldn't hear them in the taller, noisier city. The story illustrates the idea of signal-to-noise ratio. The signal of the sirens lost out to the sheer level of noise in New York.

In an increasingly secularized world, skyscrapers of doubt combined with the boundless noise of infotainment, idle talk, idle scribbling,[11] cyber traffic, and the general human "flight from God"[12] all flood the human heart with so much racket that the challenge of being still, of finding real silence, becomes more and more insurmountable. The voice of God isn't absent; it's drowned.

---

10. Taylor, *Secular Age*. For "the buffered self," 27, 37–42; for "disenchanted universe," 446–47.

11. Heidegger, *Being and Time*. For "idle talk," 211; for "idle scribbling," 212.

12. Picard, *Flight from God*, 1.

SHALŌM, PART 2

Heidegger says (to take one source of noise) the following of idle talk (which he defines as "*gossiping and passing the word along*"[13]):

> [Idle talk], by its very nature . . . is a closing-off, since to go back to the ground of what is talked about is something which it *leaves undone* . . . This closing-off is aggravated afresh by the fact that an understanding of what is talked about is supposedly reached in idle talk. Because of this, idle talk discourages any new inquiry and disputation.[14]

Idle talk is a form of noise that encloses one in a welter of hearsay that is passed along more emotionally than rationally (but without our realizing the blur). We find ourselves in yet another enclosure. Now we live in a closed universe trying to decide meaning in a closed autonomy only to find ourselves, still worse, enclosed in social structures that cocoon us from exploring beyond them.

In the next book in this series, we'll explore the effects of closed vs. open systems more deeply. For now, I simply want to shed light on the fact that the claim of many in secularity comes, despite all protestations to open-mindedness, from a triply closed system. In modernity, we increasingly think of belief in God as untenable when, in reality, openness to the *conditions* of belief in God has become intolerable. For our current purposes, the point is that holy imagination, even for a Christian believer, becomes increasingly difficult under the conditions of modernity.

This situation issues a call to the church at large to help Christians toward deconditioning from the enclosing aspects of modernity. This does not mean that we become medieval in our thinking, although some sources of Christian medieval thought—carefully scrutinized through the lenses of biblical exegesis and historical understanding—can be helpful. Again, we do not abruptly become medievalists. The greater urgency is to reopen the universe so that we become "porous,"[15] meaning that we are open now to outside influence, particularly from God. Now, being "porous," we exist in a

---

13. Heidegger, *Being and Time*, 212; his emphasis.
14. Heidegger, *Being and Time*, 213, his emphasis.
15. Taylor, *Secular Age*, 35–43.

STUCK

field of supra-cosmic revelation and are no longer disengaged from outside influences in the closed-world bunker of an impermeable autonomy. The recognition of external forces allows us to open our eyes to a larger story where good and evil are in a battle in and over us. But this is not to say it's a dualistic battle between equal and eternal forces, for good is stronger than evil. The ground for saying so is that in this larger, transcendent story, God is the king and Satan is not.

Only as we emerge from the cocoon of modernity can we revitalize the holy imagination. Only as we gaze upward to God and out of ourselves can we intuit the Real beyond the real—i.e., "the God and Father of our Lord Jesus Christ" (Eph 1:3) and sender of the Holy Spirit—can we picture ourselves as on a journey to an ever-nearer homecoming. Obviously, it does no good if we imagine this out of thin air. That's more like the secular approach: imagining meaning just because we will it, whipping it up out of nowhere (of course, the effort to do so simply indicates how we are designed for meaning, yet in a secular frame the word "designed" does not and cannot fit). The holy imagination forms its images, its "seeings," *not* out of nothing but out of a story told by someone more Real than the real of our empirical understanding. Our opening to the unseen Real heals the "schism between head and heart."[16] Trapped on the "head" side of the schism, the secularized person knows the empty loneliness of endless thinking in an agonized "waiting for Godot."[17] The thinking goes on and on, but nothing conclusive ever comes to meet it. Nor can anything meaningful come. A searchlight can find nothing in a void.

There is another schism, that between gut and heart. I'm using "gut" to stand for the unexamined, visceral passions that move us. These driving urgencies boil up from a well of desire and striving. Simply pushing up and out, they don't want to mess around with thought, reflection, analyzing. It's as if the gut—our "animal organism"[18]—responds to painful thinking by blasting through it

---

16. Payne, *Healing Presence*, 132.

17. Consult Samuel Beckett's *Waiting for Godot* for a pathos-filled exploration of the absurdity of this empty waiting.

18. Lewis, *Abolition of Man*, 35.

SHALŌM, PART 2

with its own claims. Rather than tolerate the divide between head and heart, the gut dismisses both in an irrational, heartless drive for satisfied desire.

The gut—like the isolated, secular mind—is no source of holy imagination. In fact, its picture making will be unholy: imagining revenge, imagining defeat, picturing sexual satiation of one kind or another, fantasizing about power, money, status, and so on. If, regarding empty thinking, we must emerge from the cocoon of modernity, regarding the gut, we need to climb out of the mass of the barbaric. "Barbaric" is a word formed from the attempt to capture the repeated, unintelligible sounds ("bar-bar-bar") of a foreign tongue. We can imagine the gut urgently mumbling "yum-yum-yum" as it noses about for fulfillment.

Rising above both arid thinking in the void as well as the neighing lusts of barbarism, we arrive at the heart: "At all events, for the apostle [Paul] the heart is the centre of human life and is the dominating term for personal existence."[19] It is the go-between that informs both head and gut with what C. S. Lewis calls "magnanimity"[20]—i.e., greatness of soul. What enlarges our hearts, our souls? A vision of the vast story that God tells, his saying without ceasing. All around us the story flows. As we wake up from modernity and barbarism, our hearts take in the impassioned (a holy passion) realization that a massive war unfolds over a precious artwork: the cosmos itself and the hearts of all people within it. The scale of the war dwarfs that of the two world wars of the last century. We undergo the shock of recognition, of seeing truly that we and every person we meet are being fought over. A war over art, God's art. That is the story we inhabit. And it must come to inhabit us.

Imagine you have a painting that superbly captures a beloved grandmother. She has passed away, and the painting keeps you powerfully and emotionally linked to her. Her warmth and kindness depicted wonderfully by the artist, all you have to do to feel peace is to spend some time with that painting. Suddenly someone bursts in and throws coffee on the painting! Not only that, he wants

---

19. Käsemann, *Perspectives on Paul*, 18.
20. Lewis, *Abolition of Man*, 36.

STUCK

to steal it altogether! Now you're scrapping desperately with the intruder, determined to salvage and restore her tender face.

Just so with God's creation.

We are drawn, as believers, into this combat, but, as Paul says:

> Though we walk in the flesh, we do not war according to the flesh, for the weapons of our warfare are divinely powerful for the destruction of fortresses. We are destroying speculations and every lofty thing raised up against the knowledge of God, and we are taking every thought captive to the obedience of Christ. (2 Cor 10:3–5)

In "the knowledge of God," we learn that from "the obedience of Christ" (who died and was raised) we are set free from "fortresses" and "speculations" and "lofty" things that seek to oppose that "knowledge of God." So:

- "fortresses"—any fortified complex of thought that opposes God's right to tell God's own story.
- "speculations"—any reasoning confined to the logic of a closed universe
- "lofty" things—prideful heights of hubris (like the Tower of Babel) that we use to hedge ourselves in from God.

Only as we oppose these adversaries consistently, taking our thoughts captive from them, will our holy imaginations gain ground. Otherwise, our picture-forming capacity will be tied either to the wild kiteflying of the secular mind or the "yum-yum" drumbeat of inordinate desire. Will we waste our God-given gift of imagination? Or will we take that gift back for higher use?

As to the misuse of imagination, I speak as a former sex addict who came to Christ with many pornographic images plaguing my mind. They constantly polluted my picture-forming capacity. Persistent and distressing (and tempting), they kept popping up like gas bubbles, playing havoc with my ability to walk with Christ. I remember the day (much prayer had intervened over years) when the last pornographic image left my mind, its power gone! A day of grace, liberation, God's faithfulness, thanksgiving! More and more, I was able to enter the joy of holy imagination, learning to lift my heart to Christ and let him tell me who I am. When pornography dominated my mind, I was identified as dark, twisted, addicted, overpowered. As Christ cleansed the bedeviling images out of me, I could see who I really am: standing "in Christ" as the beloved child of God, this God who refuses to be without me. I could see the cross at the center of my life, acting as both anchor and wings. Do you see the pictures forming?

I have permission to use a counseling session (disguising the identity of the counselee) to illustrate the holy imagination still more. A woman told me about a recent dream in which she was trapped in a limousine with a relative who had sexually abused her as a child. Try as she might, she could not escape. In our session, she still felt the urgency of being trapped and asked if we could pray. In the prayer, an image emerges: her belly has been cut open, and rather than there being blood running down her body, it is all pooling in the wound as if in a dark well. Still praying, she sees Christ drop a seed into the morass of her open guts. The seed takes root, and the dark mass in her abdomen turns into life-giving soil. A great tree grows out of it and captures the limo in its branches. Now the limo can't escape, and the once-inescapable impact of the abuse loosens its grip.

Much more can be made of this imagery, but the main point is that her heart (not just her head and her unfiltered desires) was able to form holy pictures that brought hope and healing. Years of prayer, Scripture reading, worship, and fellowship had formed her heart spiritually. She was able to mediate between her head and her gut to place herself before "the knowledge of God." This freshly grounded her in the transcendent, liberating story God has told, is telling, and will tell. Christ the sower casting good seed into long-standing wounds now supplements our earlier image of sending Christ to the door to refuse the messengers of despair. There are many such images from the realm of God's holiness, and they call us into the combat and to the peace beyond it.

The best atmosphere for the practices of putting on the armor of God and of holy imagination is prayer. We sit quietly before the Lord and picture ourselves putting on, piece by piece, the armor of God that Paul describes in Eph 6:10–18. This practice gains in power when we link it with Rom 13:12, 14, realizing—as we've discussed—that the armor *is* Christ and as such is light that repels darkness. We then ask God "that the eyes of [our] heart may be enlightened" (Eph 1:18) in holy imagination to help us see ourselves standing tall like antennas toward Christ, ready to hear him tell us who we are.

Conclusion

We began with a *conundrum*: How do we keep the disappointing things from becoming defining things? We moved to the *fulcrum*, the leverage of creating a vantage point *outside* the disappointing things by using founding memories from "the house of memory," the Bible. Then we felt some *momentum* building in that hope became part of the story, especially the hope in God's pursuing his shattered creation. Hope implies that we are designed for a hopeful story. But what if our life's story collides with real hopelessness? This question led us to the theme of *liberation*, where we grappled with the difference between true waiting and mere stuck-ness, learning that real waiting defeats time from within time by looking to God's end-time. Yet this is no formula that secures an easy win. We saw that life tends always toward a *pendulum* that swings back toward old, self-invented ways of coping. Trying to understand this pendulum, this backswing, we explored the impact of sin and trauma, especially the trauma that God brings to our old story. This is the trauma of the cross. To avoid that trauma, we bargain that we can live between traumas, that of God and that of self-protection. We hesitate between the two, being hypnotized by the blandishments of ordinary flourishing. We called it a *humdrum* life. In it, we slave onward, taken in by alluring but false promises. But we long for more; we long for life to be creative, to be a *poem*. The conditions for a "poetic" life are established by the work of Christ. They are: embracing God's transcendence (everything under an "open heaven"), sensing affirmation from God instead of existing in

STUCK

anxiety, and resting in God's promise of rest. These lead to a sense of *welcome*. We saw there that God pushes back chaos to create a space for us, a space of rest, creativity, and hope. In spaciousness, we have room to settle down and sense God's gladness at being our God, and we, his people. Now, in the wide-open love of God, we lean toward *shalōm*. We looked deeply into Lamentations chapter 3 to understand "the turn" that is like the breathtaking turn in a fairy tale. Didn't Mary Magdalene catch her breath when she thought she was talking to the gardener, and Jesus said her name? In naming her, Jesus revealed his love for her, revealing that he had killed death that she might live. In her, we see that *we* might live. If we really see the gift, we catch our breath. Also, we gain the *shalōm* of learning to "send Jesus to the door" by putting on the full armor of God and using our "holy imagination." The more we follow the track laid out here, the more we keep the disappointing things from becoming the defining things.

This book may certainly be read as one that stands by itself. But it doesn't stand alone. In the next book, *Cleanup*, we'll discover more about creating the conditions that strengthen, in an always-challenging world, our capacities to think, imagine, and feel within a relationship with God. We'll learn about repentance, especially, as a lifestyle of turning (yes, this is part of "the turn") from darkness to light.

Bibliography

Abbott-Smith, George. *A Manual Greek Lexicon of the New Testament*. Edinburgh: T. & T. Clark, 1973.
Allender, Dan. *To Be Told*. Colorado Springs: Waterbrook, 2005.
Augustine. *Confessions*. Oxford: Oxford University Press, 1992.
Barrett, William. *The Illusion of Technique*. Garden City, NY: Anchor, 1979.
Beckett, Samuel. *Waiting for Godot*. New York: Grove, 1954.
Benjamin, Walter. *Illuminations*. New York: Schocken, 1968.
Brueggemann, Walter. *Finally Comes the Poet*. Minneapolis: Augsburg Fortress, 1989.
———. *Hope within History*. Atlanta: John Knox, 1987.
Coles, Robert. *The Call of Stories*. Boston: Houghton Mifflin, 1989.
Crabb, Lawrence J. "School of Spiritual Direction." Unpublished lecture notes presented at the School of Spiritual Direction conference 57 of New Way Ministries, Asheville, NC, April 18–23, 2015.
Dawson, Gerrit. *Jesus Ascended*. Carlisle, NJ: Presbyterian & Reformed, 2004.
Dickens, Charles. *Hard Times*. Hertfordshire, UK: Wordsworth, 1995.
Donoghue, Denis. *Words Alone: The Poet T. S. Eliot*. New Haven: Yale University, 2000.
Ehrenreich, Barbara. *Bright-Sided*. New York: Henry Holt & Co., 2009.
Eliot, T. S. *The Waste Land*. New York: Harcourt Brace, 1922.
Elliger, Karl, and Willhelm Rudolph, eds. *Biblia Hebraica Stuttgartensia*. Stuttgart, Germany: Deutsche Bibelstiftung, 1977.
Gesenius, William. *Hebrew and Chaldee Lexicon to the Old Testament Scriptures*. Translated by Samuel Prideaux Tregelles. Grand Rapids, MI: Baker, 1979.
Ginsburg, Allen. "Howl." In *Howl and Other Poems*, 9–26. San Francisco: City Lights, 1959.
Gove, Phillip, et al., eds. Webster's Third New International Dictionary. Chicago: G. & C. Merriam, 1966.
Griffis, Rachel B. "'Not a Question of Choice': Freedom, Identity, and Place in Willa Cather's *O Pioneers!*" *Local Culture: A Journal of the Front Porch Republic* 3.1 (2021) 36–42.

BIBLIOGRAPHY

Heidegger, Martin. *Being and Time*. Translated by John Macquarrie and Edward Robinson. New York: Harper & Row, 1962.

Heschel, Abraham. *God in Search of Man*. New York: Farrar, Straus & Giroux, 1986.

Hitz, Zena. *Lost in Thought*. Princeton, NJ: Princeton University Press, 2020.

Hobbes, Thomas. *Of Man, Being the First Part of Leviathan*. Edited by Charles W. Eliot. Harvard Classics. New York: P. F. Collier and Son, 1910.

Irenaeus. *Against Heresies*. In *The Apostolic Fathers with Justin Martyr and Irenaeus*. Ante-Nicene Fathers 1. Translated by Alexander Roberts and William Rambaut. Edited by Alexander Roberts et al. Buffalo, NY: Christian Literature, 1885. http://www.newadvent.org/fathers/0103.htm.

Jones, Alan. *Soul Making: The Desert Way of Spirituality*. San Francisco: HarperCollins, 1989.

Käsemann, Ernst. *On Being a Disciple of the Crucified Nazarene*. Grand Rapids: Eerdmans, 2010.

———. *Perspectives on Paul*. Translated by Margaret Kohl. Philadelphia: Fortress, 1971.

Kaufman, Gershen. *Shame: The Power of Caring*. Rochester, VT: Schenkman, 1992.

Kierkegaard, Søren. *Fear and Trembling and the Sickness unto Death*. Garden City, NY: Anchor, 1954.

Koehler, Ludwig, et al. *The Hebrew and Aramaic Lexicon of the Old Testament*. Translated by M. E. J. Richardson. Boston: Brill, 2001.

Lewis, C. S. *The Abolition of Man*. New York: Simon & Schuster, 1996.

Liddell, Henry George, and Robert Scott. *A Greek-English Lexicon*. Unabridged. Oxford: Oxford University Press, 1940.

Lovelace, Richard. *Dynamics of Spiritual Life*. Downers Grove, IL: InterVarsity, 1979.

Malcolm, Janet. *Psychoanalysis: The Impossible Profession*. New York: Knopf, 1981.

Moltmann, Jurgen. *The Crucified God*. Translated by R. A. Wilson and John Bowden. Minneapolis: Fortress, 1993.

———. *The Spirit of Life: A Universal Affirmation*. Translated by Margaret Kohl. Philadelphia: Fortress, 2001.

O'Brien, Michael. *A Cry of Stone*. San Francisco: Ignatius, 2003.

Payne, Leanne. *The Healing Presence*. Westchester, IL: Crossway, 1989.

———. *Real Presence*. Grand Rapids: Baker, 1995.

Picard, Max. *The Flight from God*. Translated by Marianne Kuschnitzky and J. M. Cameron. Chicago: Henry Regnery, 1951.

Ricoeur, Paul. *The Conflict of Interpretations*. Evanston, IL: Northwestern University Press, 1974.

———. *Fallible Man*. New York: Fordham University Press, 1986.

———. *Freud and Philosophy*. New Haven: Yale University Press, 1970.

Scarry, Elaine. *The Body in Pain*. New York: Oxford University Press, 1985.

Schaeffer, Francis A. *No Little People*. Downers Grove, IL: InterVarsity, 1974.

BIBLIOGRAPHY

Smith, Christian. *Soul Searching: The Religious and Spiritual Lives of American Teenagers.* Oxford: Oxford University Press, 2005.

Strupp, Hans, and Jeffrey Binder. *Psychotherapy in a New Key.* New York: Basic, 1984.

Taylor, Charles. *A Secular Age.* Cambridge, MA: Harvard University Press, 2007.

———. *Sources of the Self.* Cambridge, MA: Harvard University Press, 1989.

Tolkien, J. R. R. "On Fairy Stories." In *Poems and Stories*, 113–88. Boston: Houghton Mifflin, 1994.

Trueman, Carl. *The Rise and Triumph of the Modern Self.* Wheaton, IL: Crossway, 2020.

Wolfe, Tom. *The Bonfire of the Vanities.* New York: Picador, 2008.

Wright, N. T. *The New Testament and the People of God.* Minneapolis: Fortress, 1992.

www.ingramcontent.com/pod-product-compliance
Lightning Source LLC
Chambersburg PA
CBHW070459090426
42735CB00012B/2623